Linguistic Response to the Taboo of Death in Egyptian Arabic

Magdalena Zawrotna

Linguistic Response to the Taboo of Death in Egyptian Arabic

Jagiellonian University Press

The publication of this volume was financed by the Institute of Oriental Studies – Faculty of Philology of the Jagiellonian University

Reviewer
dr hab. Marcin Grodzki

Cover design
Michał Kowalski

First edition, Kraków 2021

ISBN 978-83-233-5031-6
ISBN 978-83-233-7264-6 (e-book)

JAGIELLONIAN
UNIVERSITY
PRESS

www.wuj.pl

Jagiellonian University Press
Editorial Offices: Michałowskiego 9/2, 31-126 Kraków
Phone: +48 12 663 23 80
Distribution: Phone: +48 12 631 01 97
Cell Phone: +48 506 006 674, e-mail: sprzedaz@wuj.pl
Bank: PEKAO SA, IBAN PL 80 1240 4722 1111 0000 4856 3325

Contents

1. Transcription system

Consonants

	Bilabial	Labiodental	Dental	Alveolar	Alveopalatal	Palatal	Velar	Backvelar	Uvular	Pharyngealyn	Glottal
Stop –voicless	p		t	ṭ			k		q		ʾ
Stop – voiced	b		d	ṭ			g				
Fricative – voiceless		f	s	ṣ	š			ḫ		ḥ	h
Fricative – voiced		v	z	ẓ	ž			ġ		ʿ	
Nasal – voiced	m		n								
Lateral – voiced			l	ḷ							
Flap – voiced				r							
Semivowel – voiced	w					y					

Vowels

	Short		Long	
	Front	**Back**	**Front**	**Back**
High	i	u	ī	ū
Mid	e	o	ē	ō
Low	a		ā	

In the transcription system, the actual pronunciation is taken into account, therefore, for instance, in *ya rabb il-ʿalamīn* [ā] is shortened to [a]. Whenever there is doubt in terms of whether Egyptian Arabic (EA) or Modern Standard Arabic (MSA)/Classical Arabic (CA) pronunciation should be applied, the transcription followed a native speaker suggestion (see Methods). Most of the examples, however, represent a mixed variety.

- In dialectal material, whenever the environment of a sound calls for it, short vowels are dropped, e.g., *ya bni,* long vowels are shortened, e.g., *fakra, mugamalāt, ḥagg, šabb* and helping vowels are added.
- In line with the above, vocative *ya* is spelled with the short *a*, whereas in standard examples it is spelled conventionally as *yā*.
- Verbs with object pronouns, e.g., *yikallimhum,* nouns with possessive pronouns, e.g., *kitābu* and all word combinations in which one word is attached to another as a clitic are written together.
- The use of hyphen is highly limited, it appears mostly in the article *al-*/*il-*.
- The initial hamza is dropped when it is in a middle of a breath group and elsewhere with only a few exceptions, e.g., in which [ʾ] is the result of the reduction of [q].
- The process of emphasis spreading, e.g., the occurrence of backed allophones of [a] and [ā] is not noted.
- *Ē* in dialectal examples corresponds to the standard diphthong [ay], e.g., *ʿalēh.*
- Both *h* and *ḥ* may be used to note the future tense particle, depending on the original notation.
- In original examples the Latin spelling (if available) suggest both *yi-* and *y-* in verbal forms, therefore, in some cases short vowels were dropped, e.g., *tkūn.*
- In *aḷḷāh* the final *h* is retained in consistency with *ēh, lēh*, etc., although, in most cases, it is silent.
- The negative particle (*la, lā, laʾ*) is, for more consistency, spelled always as *lā.*
- Individual pronunciation of EA users might differ, therefore, when in doubt, the spelling was provided by a native speaker.
- In EA examples, the punctuation is limited to comas, question and exclamation marks, occasionally a colon might occur.
- In direct citations the original spelling was retained, e.g. "sheex" (Parkinson 1985: 136).
- No capitals are used in the transcription.
- MSA/CA notation is consistent with ISO transcription. In English fragments the conventional notation is employed.
- Some inconsistencies in spelling might occur when code-switching (CS) between MSA/CA and EA is employed when different situations of use are referred to, e.g., *ḥasbunā ḷḷāh wa niʿma l-wakīl*/*ḥasbina ḷḷāh wa niʿma l-wakīl.*

The notation of formulae was highly problematic, because they mostly have standard or classical origin; however, the usage is dialectal, e.g., *subḥāna l-ḥayy allaḏi lā yamūt, aḷḷāh yirḥamak ya ʿamm ḥasan, yatagāwaz ʿan sayʾātu.* Consultations with a native speaker did not always solve the problem, because often several variants of pronunciation were proposed. Therefore, in such cases the following rule was adopted: when the rest of the utterance is unambiguously classical, the notation follows ISO rules with *ğ* for ج, dental sounds and other markers of the standard variant. Otherwise, the pronunciation was recognised as dialectal. In some cases, however, two types of notation (and pronunciation) are adopted, based on the intuition of the consulted native speaker.

2. Introduction

Human beings are fearful creatures. The world that surrounds them is full of dangers. They fear death in particular, and therefore, seek protection from danger and the ubiquitous possibility of dying. Although this is common for all people, this book focuses on Egyptians, their fears and their sociocultural conditions.

Fear is perceived in Islam[1] as a natural reaction to the surrounding world; people are fearful because they were created this way. According to the Quran, *inna l-insāna ḫuliqa halūʿan* 'man was created anxious' (Piamenta 1979: 19). So, people fear "physical, mental, and spiritual oddities, bad actions, adversities and misfortunes, demonic and evil forces" (Piamenta 1979: 92). There is a potential danger in everything, therefore, people, when overwhelmed by uncertainty, or when confronted with death, illness, loss of a precious possession, etc., seek refuge in God, beg for God's mercy or express their resignation to God's will:

(1) *ana fi ʿarḍi rabbina* 'I implore the protection of our Lord' (MP)[2].

(2) *ana mitwakkil ʿala ḷḷāh* 'I have put my trust in God' (MP).

(3) *ḥasbuna ḷḷāh wi niʿma l-wakīl* 'God is sufficient for us. Most excellent is he in whom we trust' (MP).

(4) *ḫallīha ʿala ḷḷāh* 'Leave it to God!' (MP).

(5) *iḥna ʾulna lli ʿalēna wi l-bāʾi ʿala ḷḷāh* 'We have said whatever we should; the rest depends on God' (MP).

By reciting these formulae, people submit themselves to God's will, hoping that God will save them from danger. They do not have to be explicit about their fears, for they are often a subject of taboo. Various methods of indirectness are used to circumvent a dangerous topic. In such cases, the way it is communicated reflects

1 The data in this book come mostly from Muslims with only a few samples from Christians.

2 Sources of the quotations in this work are: MP = Moshe Piamenta (1979), DS = Devin Stewart (1996), FAS = Fatma Abdel Samad (1990), AW = Alison Wray (2002), MW = Manfred Woidich (1995, 2018).

cultural identity and beliefs. In this book, I present an analysis of the reaction to the taboo of death, which can probably be considered as one of the greatest dangers in store for people in life and in society.

The first author to use the term "taboo" (Polynesian *tapu*) was Captain James Cook in the logbook of his third trip to Polynesia 1776–1779, on his voyage to discover the Northwest Passage from the Atlantic to the Pacific (Allan and Burridge 2006: 3). He had been observing the behaviour of Tahitians for several years noticing that there were types of food, places and actions that seemed to be forbidden. Since Captain Cook's times the word "taboo" has become widespread and the concept has been repeatedly defined. It is assumed that taboo is a prohibition associated with a certain object or action. However, taboo is also the very object or person to whom it applies. This twofold understanding of the word "taboo" persists in modern languages, e.g., we often say that money is "taboo" in Western culture, but it is also "taboo" to talk about money. In primitive cultures taboo proscriptions applied to people, activities, places and behaviours that were in some way unusual or incomprehensible, and thus aroused fear or admiration. These include, e.g., restrictions on pronouncing the name of the ruler and the gods or proscription on touching the ruler. The element of fear seems to be an important aspect of taboo – the sense of fear is related to the awareness of danger associated with certain objects. Steiner (1967) views the notion of taboo as a part of those situations in which attitudes to values manifest themselves in the form of danger:

> Social relations are describable in terms of danger; through contagion there is social participation in danger. And we find expressed in the same term, those of taboo, two quite separate social functions: (1) the classification and identification of transgressions (which is associated with, though it can be studied apart from, processes of social learning), and (2) the institutional localization of danger, both by the specification of the dangerous and by the protection of society from endangered, and hence dangerous, persons (Steiner 1967: 147).

The expression: "taboo" has caused Western researchers many difficulties, mainly because it comes from a culture foreign to them. It is very meaning, which combines implications of sacredness and prohibition, is problematic. Such duality can be also seen in the Hebrew concept of *qodeš*, Latin *sacer* or Arabic *ḥarām*. According to Sigmund Freud (1918: 22), taboo as a notion was shaped at a specific moment in the history of civilisation, when the concepts of awe and aversion were not yet separated. He suggests that sanctity and danger have a common root. Steiner notes that the meanings of sacred and forbidden appear in many Polynesian languages (Steiner 1967: 33), and the distinction between these terms was introduced post factum (Steiner 1967: 34). The author further explains that the way to understand the relation between these terms would be to assume the existence of a triad of concepts: the sacred, the prohibited, the unclean (where the sacred and the unclean do not connect with each other, but both are derived from the prohibited; therefore, the prohibited would be the central principle with the sacred and the unclean as extensions of it (Steiner 1967: 35). Robertson-Smith (1894) came up with another idea on how to combine together the concepts of sanctity and prohibition. According to him, the middle term would be the consecration of a thing/action/person that takes place to limit man's rights towards it (Steiner 1967: 72). Prohibition is always associated with danger. For the Polynesian people, it was the danger that marked the boundaries of the ban, both in relation to the sacred and the unclean. "The Polynesian, for example, does not think of a chief or a temple as holy and a corpse as unclean. He thinks of them all as things dangerous" (Steiner 1967: 120). The taboo constituted a rule to "hedge the divinity off" (Douglas 1966: 18). The idea of separation (of what pertains to God and people) is clear in the Hebrew root Q-D-Š (*ibid.*). Frazer also comments on this matter when describing Syrian prohibitions: "Some said it was because pigs were unclean; others said it was because pigs were sacred. This points to a hazy state of religious thought in which ideas of sanctity and uncleanness are not yet sharply distinguished, both being blent in a sort of vaporous solution to which we give the name taboo" (Frazer 1911: 23), as well as in: "Taboos of sanctity agree with taboos of pollution, because in the savage mind the ideas of sanctity and pollution are not yet differentiated" (Frazer 1911: 224). Yet another attempt to combine the two concepts is by Radcliffe Brown, who introduces the term "ritual value" (Steiner 1967: 122). Such a value would characterise behaviours towards objects that are the subjects of rites (sacralisation, avoidance, respect).

Qanbar (2011) classifies death as a macrolinguistic taboo, claiming that expressions related to it are unmentionable, because speakers tend to avoid verbalising their fears. Some of the methods of coping with the awareness of the inevitability of death are rituals of mourning, refinement and ennoblement. Some of them serve both the function of mitigation the fear of death as well as consolation after the death of people's loved ones. The ritualisation of behaviour associated with death includes death ceremonies, funerals, condolences and prayers. However, in a previous study on Egyptian society conducted in 2016 I found out that the tabooisation of death appears to be a more complex issue[3]. It turns out that death is not a taboo, as long as it does not concern one of the participants in the communication directly. In that particular project I studied taboos in Egyptian linguistic politeness, based on a large corpus of text from online communication. The study included a large collection of conversations about death with no signs of hedging, where the most preferable strategy was directness:

[3] The results of the study remain unpublished.

(6) *mōt fi s-sittīn miš wiḥiš, huwwa il-wāḥid lāzim yi'īš alf sana?* 'Death at the age of 60 doesn't feel like a bad idea, who said everyone has to live a 1000 years?'

(7) (a) *gatkum il-bala! ana dāḫil anām wi ya rabb ma-ṣḥāš* 'Go to hell! [may the disaster afflict you] I'm going to sleep, and I hope [oh Lord] I will never wake up'.
(b) *lēh kida ya 'amm il-ḥagg?* 'Why so, uncle pilgrim?'
(c) *bi'id iš-šarr, wi mīn hayišrif 'alayya ana wi l-'ayyil waldak?* '[God] dismiss the evil, who is going to take care of me and the boy, your son?'
(d) *bass mat'ulš kida, haz'al asāsan if you die* 'Stop, don't say that, I will be very sad if you die'.
(e) *ya 'amm istanna, gīb il-fulūs illi 'alēk il-awwil* 'Uncle, wait a moment, I want my money back first'.

Death seen as a distant event was sometimes the subject of jokes as in *ya 'amm istanna, gīb il-fulūs illi 'alēk il-awwil* 'uncle, wait a moment, I want my money back first' or *bi'id iš-šarr, wi mīn hayišrif 'alayya ana wi l-'ayyal waldak?* '[God] dismiss the evil. Who is going to take care of me and the boy, your son?'. Hedging in the form of prophylactic formulae occurs rarely and usually as a joke, as in: *bi'id iš-šarr* '[God] dismiss the evil'.

However, when death concerns the speaker personally, no jokes are admissible, rather, formulae with reference to God are used. As can be seen in the next example, when a person seriously fears death or when death afflicts someone, the following mitigating strategies are used: embellishing the death by using euphemisms: *rāḥit li makān aḥsan* 'she's gone to a better place' or *itwaffit* 'passed away', which is a highly conventionalised form. Additionally, the minimiser *ma'lēš* is used to mean "don't worry" almost always with a further explanation, e.g., emphasising that the deceased person is in a better place. We find the expression *in šā' aḷḷāh* 'God willing' uttered after conveying blessing or expressing hope for an action to be performed by God. Such prophylactic formulae as e.g. *bi'id iš-šarr* '(may God) dismiss the evil' are employed when the danger of death is mentioned.

(8) (a) *kull yōm bab'a mar'ūb bi l-lēl wana mrawwaḥ wi l-mikrubāṣ byiṭīr zayy il-magnūn li amūt, ba'd ḫabar maryam ḥāsis innu miš far'a, ṭab mamūt ēh ya'ni* 'Every night I feel terrified that I might die while coming back from work and the microbus flies around like crazy, but after the information about Maryam I feel that there is no point in it, OK, I will die, so what?'
(b) *bi'id iš-šarr 'annak in šā' aḷḷāh* '[God] dismiss from you the evil, God willing'.

(9) (a) *hiba rāḥit is-sama, rabbina yi'zi ahlaha wi yi'zīna 'ala fura'ha, iṣ-ṣala 'alēha bi masgid is-salām bi madinit naṣr ba'd ṣalāt il-gum'a* 'Hiba went to heaven, may our Lord console her family and console us after this loss,

the prayer for her soul will be in the Salam Mosque in Nasr City after the Friday prayer'[4].
(b) *ēh illi ḥaṣal* 'What happened?'
(a) *bint ṣaḥbitna ʿamalit hadsa wi twaffit* 'Our friend had a car accident and passed away'.
(b) *rabbina yiʿzīku* 'May our Lord console you'.
(c) *lā ilāha illa ḷḷāh, rabbina yirḥamha wi yiṣabbarku* 'There is no deity but God, may our Lord have mercy on her and give you patience'.
(d) *rabbina yiʿzīk, maʿlēš rāḥit li makān aḥsan, in šāʾ aḷḷāh* 'May our Lord console you, don't worry, she's gone to a better place'.

In conversations about illness, the same tendency is visible. There is a difference in how speakers announce light versus serious illness and react to it. The information about light illness involves the use of intensifiers and in response blessings are preferred over other strategies, e.g., giving advice, joking. The information about serious disease that could probably be fatal requires the use of hedging, nonconventional indirectness and off-record; for instance, requests for prayers are often used in this function. When apprehending serious illness, speakers resort to God by praising him as the possessor of healing powers. It seems, however, that the crucial feature of response to the taboo of death is formulaicity.

Taboo is discharged verbally. There are plentiful examples of this in various cultures of the world. In Ghana and Togo, the speakers of Ewe are obliged to use their right hand for transactions, but when for some reason the left hand is used, they use the formula *Mia [ló]!* 'Left hand!' to indemnify the action. The response to it: *Así-é!* 'It is a hand!' confirms that the taboo was averted (Ameka 1987: 321). In the Arab world the danger might come from the relation between speakers; jealousy is believed to bring misfortune, in particular. Even sincere and well-intended compliments may be portentous and ominous. "Laudatory expressions may attract the contrary of what they propose to say, because envy may be mixed with them. That is why a mother is not simply told that her son is handsome and healthy, or a proprietor that his house is splendid. It is feared that the son might fall sick and the house might burn. Consequently, a pious formula, thought to annihilate the bad magic effect of praise accompanies the compliment – *Allah yihfazu* (God protect him) or *Ism Allah ʿaleyh* (God's name on him)" (Hamady 1960: 166).

When Egyptians fear death or apprehend it, or while comforting the addressee on the occasion of someone's death, they use a number of formulae, some of them prophylactic, others aiming to soothe the person. Bringing up such strongly tabooed subjects as death is an act of threat to the positive and negative aspects of both

[4] The current example is a conversation in a mixed Christian – Muslim group.

the speaker's and addressee's face[5]. The verse 2:156 of *Surah Al-Baqara* known as "a supplication in times of hardship" is "recommended" when a misfortune overtakes a man or when disaster strikes him/her:

(10) *innā li llāh wa innā ilayhi rāǧiʿūn* 'Verily to God we belong and unto him is our return'.

Calamities and disasters such as someone's death are considered a test or a trial, which, when transversed, bring a great reward. People should, therefore, accept them with full confidence and trust in God's plans. Moreover, ambivalence is frequently emphasised when consoling a person; a reference is made to the reward stored in Heaven for a person who withstands all earthly suffering, and to the belief that the deceased person is currently in a better place. Condolences (*taʿziya*) may take the form *duʿā'* (prayers, invocations addressed to God asking for blessings), most of which are highly conventionalised. A wide but not unlimited lexicon is employed to react to the information about death. In the material studied earlier in 2016, a striking fact was that personal utterances were extremely rare and non-conventionality was almost always manifested by using a solemn tone, in which references to the Quran and religious traditions were made.

The role that religion plays in everyday social interactions of Egyptians as a regulator of human relations cannot be overemphasised. Whenever people interact, they express their attitudes to the world, as well as to God and other people by defining their roles in conversation with others and highlighting their submission to God. By invocations addressed to God, they attest to their dependency on him, and through the way they address other people, they "make statements about their social universe" (Parkinson 1985: 220). In this light it is not surprising that the references to God are ubiquitous in Egypt. Such phrases as: "God is great", "praise God", "may God preserve", "to everyone the fate God gives him", "God is there", "God cuts the cold to the size of the blanket" are a part of the daily exchange almost organically woven into every conversation. It is difficult to imagine a natural interaction between two Egyptians without reference to God. Even in the simplest exchange:

(11) (a) *izzayyak?* 'How are you?'
(b) *ḥamdi llāh* 'God be praised'.

The answer to the question is presupposed, what is explicitly expressed is the gratitude to God. It is conversationally required to praise God upon hearing about the

5 Brown and Levinson (1987:13) explain "Central to our model is a highly abstract notion of 'face' which consists of two specific kinds of desires ('facewants') attributed by interactants to one another: the desire to be unimpeded in one's actions (negative face), and the desire (in some respects) to be approved of (positive face)."

interlocutor's recovery from illness, termination of travel, successful completion of a certain task, especially one involving danger. A failure to do so might be considered rude or simply unnatural. The Arab at every turn demonstrates his/her faith in God and calls his name frequently during most daily endeavours, especially at the start of various activities, which is to ensure the successful completion of the task. One of the most frequent: *aḷḷāhu akbar* 'God is the greatest' is an exclamation occurring spontaneously in the everyday life of Egyptians on various occasions (also as prosaic as walking in the streets of Cairo); it is often inscribed on the walls of the city, murals and graffiti. As Patai notices in the Arab world: "The name of God is invoked with the same readiness in the course of quarrels. The stronger the quarrel, the larger the group, which God is asked to curse. From 'May God curse your ancestors!' and finally, 'May God curse your religion!' or even 'May God curse your Muhammad' (Patai 1973: 159). The vehicles traversing the streets of Cairo carry multicoloured stickers with *basmala*, *ḥamdala*[6] and other expressions written on them, with an aim to protect the driver from the dangers of the road and misfortunes of bad traffic. God's name can be heard everywhere and all the time. "The most usual exclamation at hearing or seeing something surprising and exciting is *waḷḷāhi* 'by God'" (*ibid.*). God is present throughout a person's life and in all his/her actions; whatever they do; they should mention the name of God. According to Piamenta (1979: 20), God's name "is said to be *lafẓ al-jalāla* 'the word of majesty', or *al-ism al-a'ẓam* 'the great name', and *ism al-dhat*, 'name of the Divine Substance (essence or person)". In the Quran *aḷḷāh* appears several hundred times, whereas there is not a single occurrence of the definite: *ar-rabb* 'the Lord' (*ibid.*). On the other hand, in daily life, the form *rabbi* 'my Lord' or *rabbina* 'our Lord' is the one most often invoked.[7] The Quranic *yā rabb al-'ālamīn* 'o Lord of [all] the worlds!' is also often met in everyday speech (*ibid.*). The vocative form of *aḷḷāh* (with the particle *yā/ya*) many a time is replaced by *aḷḷāhumma* 'oh, God!' (Piamenta 1979: 51). It is probably due to the fact that *yā aḷḷāh* has undergone a semantic change and it serves as an exclamation used to encourage people to do something, to hasten them, and hurry them up (*yaḷḷa*). The word *aḷḷāh* is pronounced in accordance with the context and may include: with or without the initial disjunctive hamza (i.e. glottal stop), with long or short vowel [a], with or without emphasis on [l], with different types of intonation:

(12) *ḥamdi llah* 'Praise be to God'.
(13) *waḷḷāhi* 'Really'.
(14) *in šā' aḷḷāh* 'God willing'.
(15) *inšalla* 'At least'.

6 For explanation see below.
7 In Egypt the latter is widespread.

In many dialects of Arabic *ism aḷḷāh* 'the name of God' is an expression of excitement, apprehension, wish, surprise or admiration, and is sometimes used to calm a frightened person or a crying baby (Piamenta 1979: 64). Piamenta says, *zikr* means remembrance of God, but also calling his name and the tireless repetition of it (1979: 20). It is believed that the Prophet Muhammad said:

(16) *ḏikru ḷḷāhi šifā'u l-qulūb* 'Remembering God is a remedy for one's soul' (MP).

God commanded Prophet Muhammad to remember God, and any action performed without mentioning his name at the beginning was not to be blessed by God (Piamenta 1979: 32). Hamady notes that the Arabs always mention the name of God, whether in the public sphere or at home, alone (1960: 157). Using the name of God is generally highly advisable in Islam in the practices of *tasmiyya* 'naming', above-mentioned 'remembering', *basmala* (the utterance *bi smi ḷḷāhi r-raḥmāni r-raḥīm* 'in the name of God, the Merciful, the Compassionate!'), as well as expressions of confidence in and reliance on God (Piamenta 1979: 32). At the same time, it is forbidden to mention God's name during a visit to the toilet, in moments of anger, during sexual intercourse (Piamenta 1979: 21). In addition to *aḷḷāh* and *rabbina*, God is often referred to by one of his attributes, most of which are the so-called ninety-nine beautiful names of God. Addressing God with one of his attributes has a pragmatic function, e.g., in asking for forgiveness one may call God "the forgiver". Stewart notices that such names refer not simply to God, but specifically to his capacity to grant the petition at hand: "These tag-phrases represent an address to God that asks for a positive response to prayer or invocation" (Stewart 1996: 173). To name only a few:

(17) *wakīl* 'Trustee' as in the Quranic phrase: *'ala kulli šay'in wakīl* 'God is administrator over all thing' (MP).
(18) *raḥīm* 'Merciful'(MP).
(19) *'alīm* 'Omniscient' (MP).
(20) *laṭīf* 'Mild' (MP).
(21) *'afuww* 'Pardoner' (MP).
(22) *ġafūr/ġaffār* 'Forgiver' (MP).
(23) *mu'min* 'Safeguard' (MP).
(24) *al-bāqi* 'Immortal' (MP).

Religious utterances in Arabic involve exclamations and other fixed expressions often with a Quranic origin. They form the basis of language etiquette in Egypt. Their knowledge is a compulsory part of the linguistic competence of a speaker. They might function as blessings or protection from danger, and in this sense are considered to hold an active power. However, they are also elements of Egyptian linguistic courtesy and as such are required as tension soothers and conversational lubricants. Below are the most common expressions used in everyday life, as listed in (Piamenta 1979):

a) *basmala*

The formula: *bi smi ḷḷāhi r-raḥmāni r-rahīm* 'in the name of God, the Merciful, the Compassionate!' – one of the most often met of all prophylactic formulae against evil influences (Hamady 1960: 168), considered so powerful that it can cure the sick (Hamady 1960: 178–179). *Basmala* should be invoked at any opportunity and for any daily endeavour. If someone happens to forget to invoke *basmala* at the beginning of an action, he/she should make sure to pronounce it at the end. According to Piamenta (1979: 35), *basmala* should be said in the following instances: prior to the recitation of the Quran, when introducing rituals, when signing a contract, on entering a mosque, when opening a book or a letter, when getting into a car, when setting out on a (long) journey by air, by train or vehicle, and before eating and drinking. The formula has the function of protecting the interactants from demonic powers and in this sense is so common that one of euphemistic expressions used for such powers is 'those [whom one evades by pronouncing:] "in the name of God"' (Piamenta 1979: 6).

(25) (a) *gōzi law šafni u ana kida* 'But if my husband sees me like this...'.
(b) *wi ēh illi hayigīb gōzik hina?* 'What the hell is going to bring your husband here?'
(a) *bala'īh 'uddāmi fi kulli ḥitta zayy bi smi ḷḷāhi r-rahmāni r-rahīm* 'I see him facing me everywhere, like "basmala" (instead of "demon")' (MP).

Basmala in the perception of Egyptians can safeguard the successful completion of an activity, although not invoking it can – in certain situations – lead to exposure to danger; for example, when eating one should start with pronouncing *basmala*, otherwise, as the saying goes: "Satan joins you in eating; before you eat, he eats. There is no blessing in your food" (Piamenta 1979: 35). For some, pronouncing *basmala* is a religious duty.

b) *ism aḷḷāh (ismalla)* 'God's name'

The name of God functions in everyday language as a protective shield against what arouses fear in man, such as illness or the evil eye. In the optative sense, it may be translated, as suggested by Piamenta (1979: 14), as: "may it not befall you". According to Stewart, the name has magical powers of defense against "attacks from outside force" (Stewart 1996: 170). Furthermore, it provides protection from human and supernatural (for example genie, demons) forces; if used in conversation, it saves the addressee from harm (*ibid.*).

c) *tahlīl*
The formula: *lā ilāha ʾillā ḷḷāh* 'there is no deity but God' is used in moments of danger or the apprehension of any kind of ill-favoured developments. On the other hand, it can express admiration and amazement.

d) *ḥamdala*
Egyptians use the formula: *al-ḥamdu li llāh (il-ḥamdu li llāh, ḥamdi llāh)* 'praise be to God' in most cases to express thanks to God when asked about their well-being, also to express their gratitude to God for someone's safety. However, as a precautionary formula it can be also used in times of danger, when fearing death or sinister influence of the supernatural.

e) *istiġfār*
The formula: *astaġfiru ḷḷāh* 'I seek God's forgiveness' is used to ask forgiveness for the living and the dead when, among many other examples, confronted with the danger of the evil eye and as a precautionary measure against all kinds of bad influence; also, to chase away demons and sinister powers (Piamenta 1979: 38); in moments of fear: when, for example, passing urine in desolate places (Piamenta 1979: 6); or when complimented because of the courtesy of the interlocutor (Piamenta 1979: 141).

f) *istirǧāʿ*
The formula: *ʾastirǧiʿ* 'I seek refuge [in God]' Used in moments of strong fear, life-threatening situations when one is forced to talk about death (Piamenta 1979: 11).

g) *ḥawqala*
The formula: *lā ḥawl wa lā quwwa illā bi ḷḷāh* 'there is no power and no strength save in God' is used when in tough situations, in the face of disaster, illness, death, misery, frustration, astonishment, evil omen.

h) *istiʿāḏa*
Istiʿāḏa includes saying the following expressions in order to seek refuge in God against all possible evil influences including demons (*ibid.*).
(27) *aʿūḏu bi ḷḷāh* 'God protect/save me from that!/God forbid!' (MP).
(28) *iyāḏan bi ḷḷāh* 'God protect/save me from that!/God forbid!' (MP).
(29) *maʿāḏa(t) aḷḷāh* 'God protect/save me from that!/God forbid!' (MP).
(30) *il-ʿūḏ bi ḷḷāh* 'God protect/save me from that!/God forbid!' (MP).

This group is considered to be a highly effective "spell" used against the evil and the frightful. Inscribed on amulets (so-called *taʿwīḏ*) they have the function of protecting the bearer from lunacy (Piamenta 1979: 92). Egyptians use them most often when confronted with sin against Islam, disregard for the religious rules and regulations, blasphemy, apostasy, paganism, or unbelief. The following formula is applied after the entrance to the mosque for the ritual cleaning and with the aim to secure freedom from distraction (*ibid.*).

(26) *a'ūḏu bi ḷḷāhi min aš-šayṭān ir-rağīm* 'I seek refuge in God from Satan the outcast'.

i) *satr*

Satr means 'a shield' (a screen between man and danger) against "anxiety, and real or imaginary fear-evoking stimuli: sexual fears and taboos, extremes, moral and physical injuries, disease and death, the occult, hell, and evil society" (Piamenta 1979: 92). It is connected with the idea of God as a natural shield protecting people in every situation that gives rise to anxiety and fear. God's protection is requested by exclaiming:

(27) *rabbina yustur* 'God forbid!'

j) *taḫliyya*

The formula *aḷḷāh yiḫallīk* 'may God preserve you' provides protection from evil, misfortune and injuries. In wishing someone God's *taḫliyya* people primarily hope that God extends their interlocutor's life and protect him/her against all danger. Often, this formula is used within families, for example in conversations about children, etc.

(28) *aḷḷāh yiḫallihumlik!* 'May God preserve them [children] for you'.

k) *ḥirāsa*

Ḥirāsa is a group of formulae asking for God's guardianship. People desire that God be the guardian of themselves and their loved ones in the moments of danger. The usage of this particular group of expressions is concerned mostly with travelling to remote places, e.g., abroad. Also, the participle *il-maḥrūs* 'the guarded one' is often added after child's name to obstruct the influence of the evil eye (Piamenta 1979: 119).

(29) *ism in-nabi ḥarsak* 'May the name of the Prophet guard you!' (MP).

(30) *rabbina yuḥrusu* 'God guard him' (MP).

Instead of *yuḥrus*, a synonymic *yiḥmi* can be used:

(31) *rabbina yiḥmīkum li ba'ḍ wi lā yiwarrīna wiḥiš fīkum abadan* 'May our Lord protect and preserve you for each other, and may he never show us evil befalling you!' (MP).

l) *ḥifẓ*
Ḥāfiẓ 'preserver', one of the ninety-nine beautiful names of God, is used in the face of danger and whenever preservation is needed. Like other formulae it is a spell-like incantation, resorted to with hope that it will bring security and protection against the attacks of sinister powers (Piamenta 1979: 114).
(32) (a) *ḥāfiẓ ʿala nafsak ya bni* 'Take care of yourself, son!'
(b) *il-ḥāfiẓ aḷḷāh, ya ba* 'The Protector is God, father!' (MP).

m) *salāma*
This is used mainly to express thanks to God for someone's safety, well-being, or health.
(33) (a) *ḥamdillah ʿala s-salāma* 'Thank God for your well-being!'
(b) *aḷḷāh yisallimak* 'May God keep you safe, sound and healthy!'
(34) (a) *alf salāma ʿalēk* 'A thousand thanks to God for your safety!'
(b) *aḷḷāh yisallimak* 'May God keep you safe, sound and healthy!'
(35) (a) *salamtak* 'I wish you a speedy recovery'.
(b) *aḷḷāh yisallimak* 'May God keep you safe, sound and healthy!'
(36) (a) *salāmit iš-šūf* '[I wish] recovery to [your] sight'.
(b) *aḷḷāh yisallimak* 'May God keep you safe, sound and healthy!' (MP).

n) *amāna*
When taking refuge in God, man resorts to a group of formulae that can be seen as a contemporary manifestation of linguistic magic. Some are protective incantations with broad pragmatic usage and functions, while others are groups of notions referring to the perception of God and his relation to man. God above all grants man *amāna* 'protection', 'safeguard' (synonymous to *amān*), which can be more broadly understood as good health, security, safeness, freedom from fear, confidence, satisfaction and high spirit (Piamenta 1979: 124). In modern parlance, there is a difference in meaning between *amān* and *amāna*; "*amān* signifies security, safety; peace; shelter; protection; safeguarding, assurance of protection; indemnity, immunity from punishment; whereas *amāna* signifies reliability, trustworthiness; loyalty, faithfulness, fidelity, fealty; integrity, honesty; confidence, trust, good faith; deposition in trust; trusteeship" (Piamenta 1979: 124). Another word based on the root ʾ-M-N is related to the meaning of submission to the will of God: *imān* 'faith'. In everyday language, the expression: *amānit aḷḷāh* serves both to bless and to resort to God when exposed to danger, taboo subjects or evil influences:
(37) *fi amānit aḷḷāh/bi amānit aḷḷāh* 'Under God's protection' (MP).

Piamenta (1979: 125) notes that this expression may be added to suggestions, requests, or questions to secure fortunate communication and protection for him/herself from the sinister influences that might result from any interactions. *Amān* and *amāna* have the power to soothe and calm people when worried. This is illustrated by Piamenta with the example of a girl fearing the violation of her female honour when meeting a male stranger.

(38) *ʿalēki l-ʾamān* 'You are under protection' (MP).

The communication is a rule-governed behaviour, and it is conditioned by the norms of social convention. According to Parkinson, "[i]f a speaker is to use the terms at all (and he must by EA rules) then he must use them in a certain way, and no matter which way he chooses he is saying something" (1985: 220). Choosing not to take part in conversational rituals of everyday life, e.g., not to use the formula required by a situation, is probably the most marked choice. Also not answering formulae is marked (usually as rude), to illustrate this, Stewart quotes a common Egyptian saying: "*ruddu s-salām ya-hl alla* 'return a greeting, o people of God'" (1996: 174).

Among the examples related to the taboo of death, Piamenta quotes a great number originating from Egypt. The vast majority of them are formulaic and refer to God and religious matters. For instance, when fearing death, one says:

(39) *kafa aḷḷāh iš-šarr* 'God repel evil' (MP).

(40) *ya sātir!* 'Oh, Coverer!'

(41) *aḷḷāhumma satrak ya rabb wi ḥusn il-ḫitām* 'O, God, [cover me by] your protection! O Lord, [may my own life] end well!' (MP).

Or when apprehending death, one says as well:

(42) (a) *byiʾūlu ʿišrīn bēt* 'It is said [that] twenty houses (have been crashed by the raid)'.
(b) *rabbina yirḥamna bi raḥmitu* 'God have mercy on us!' (MP).

(43) (a) *kida sibtaha timūt?* 'Why did you let her die?'
(b) *amr rabbina* '[It was] the command of our Lord' (i.e. he wished it so) (MP).

(44) *il-ʾisma kida, rabbina ʿāyiz kida* 'This is [my] fate. Our Lord wishes it so' (MP).

(45) *ʾatalūh, aʿūzu bi ḷḷāh* 'They killed him! My God!' (MP).

(46) *raḥamkum aḷḷāh* 'May God have mercy on you!' (MP).

(47) *alf raḥma tirḥamak ya ḥagg ḥamīd, ya ḫusāra, il-mōt mayaḫudši illa š-šāṭir* 'May a thousand mercies [of God] have mercy on you, o Ḥagg Ḥamīd! What a loss! Death does not take but the smart one' (MP).

When consoling people in Egypt one wishes them long life, patience, and God's mercy. Also, trust in God, confidence in his judgments and the necessity to accept the fact that every man is mortal are highlighted:

(48) *rabbina yiṣabbarak* 'May God give you patience!' (MP).

(49) *kullina li l- mōt* 'All of us unto death' (MP).
(50) *raḥimahu ḷḷāh wa innā li ḷḷāhi wa innā ilayhi rāǧiʿūn* 'God have mercy on him and verily, we are God's and to God we will return' (MP).
(51) *rabbina yiddīki ṭūlit il-ʿumr ya mʿallima kullina ḥanmūt maḥaddiš byiʿammar abadan ġēr il-ʿamal il-kuwayyis* 'May our Lord grant you longevity, lady [lit. woman teacher]! All of us are going to die. No one lasts save a good deed' (MP).
(52) *aḷḷāh yiġfir zunūbu* 'May God forgive his sins' (MP).
(53) *il-baʾiya li ḷḷāh* 'The existence is God' (MP).
(54) *lā ḥawl wa lā quwwa illa bi ḷḷāh* 'There is no power and no strength save in God' (MP).
(55) *ḥayātak il-baʾya* 'May you live long [lit. your life is what remains' (MP).
(56) (a) *il-baʾiya fi ḥayātak* 'Your life is what remains'.
(b) *aḷḷāh yimidd bi ḥayātak* 'May God prolong your life!' (MP).

Formulae, especially those related to God are ubiquitous in Egyptian Arabic and have multiple pragmatic roles in all everyday situations to the extent that they undergo automatisation, and sometimes become grammaticised in their functions. The following examples both mean "please", although the first is structurally a constative utterance: "I am kissing your hands", and the second one is a blessing: "may God preserve you".
(57) *abūs īdak* 'Please'.
(58) *aḷḷāh yiḥallīk* 'Please'.

In the current material, the invocation *ya rabb* 'oh, Lord' was so ubiquitous, one can assume that it has a similar function of saying "please" or, on other occasions, of confirmation.

One of the functions of using formulae is euphemisation in taboo-marked communicative situation. Therefore, instead of naming the dangerous object or event, a formula referring to God might be used, as in the example cited before.
(59) *balāʾīh ʿuddāmi fi kulli ḥitta zayyi bi smi ḷḷāhi r-rahmāni r-rahīm* 'I see him facing me everywhere, like "*basmala*"' (MP).

Invocations addressed to God may at times replace the tabooed events in their entirety, for example, instead of reporting in detail on a sin committed by a person (which may be dangerous to the speaker), one of the formulae denoting recourse to God may be used.
(60) *kafar wi l-ʿiyāz bi ḷḷāh* 'He has blasphemed and "the refuge in God"' (MP).

The expression "the refuge in God" replaces all other types of committed sins, about which the speaker does not want to think or speak. Similarly, the very invocation of *basmala* may express anxiety, fear or surprise; therefore, expressing them explicitly becomes needless, for example, when seeing someone being injured:

(61) *bi smi ḷḷāhi r-raḥmāni r-raḥīm, ism aḷḷāh'alēk* 'Oh! I hope you are not hurt' (MP).

The basic principle in Egyptian politeness, as in many others, is the indirectness of communication. Certain speech acts may constitute a threat to the image of speakers or cause disturbance to the interlocutors; therefore, they are substituted by other, less imposing ones. This usually results in breaching one or more of the conversational maxims, which leads to the emergence of an implicature (marking politeness). Most of the implicatures that result from such a substitution are conventionalised and used automatically. When an Egyptian makes a request, a common practice is to perform a blessing or to wish the interlocutor good health instead of asking explicitly by saying "please" (63). This involves the "exchange of goods" (*ma'rūf*), characteristic for Arab culture. The formulae and blessings with a reference to God described earlier have various pragmatic functions, e.g., the formula *aḷḷāh yiḫallīk* is used in greetings, wishes, thanks, congratulations, condolences, etc.

(62) (a) *ahlan, izzayyak?* 'Welcome! How are you?'.
(b) (answering in reverence:) *aḷḷāh yiḫallīk ya sa'adit il-bēh* 'May God preserve you, your Grace!' (MP).

Also, the formula *aḷḷāh yiḥfiẓak* 'may God preserve you' is used to express thanks for good wishes, blessings, condolences, greetings, congratulations, complement, questions about the health (Piamenta 1979: 113).

(63) (a) *tiṣbaḥ 'ala ḫēr* 'Good night!' [lit. "May you wake well in the morning'].
(b) *fi ḥifẓi ḷḷāhbi ḥifẓ rabbina* '[Go] under God's protection!' (MP).
(64) (a) *di furṣa sa'īda 'awi* 'It has been a happy occasion'.
(b) *aḷḷāh yiḥfiẓak* 'Thank you!' (MP).
(65) (a) *intu nās ṭayyibīn* 'You are nice people'.
(b) *aḷḷāh yiḫallīk* 'May God preserve you!' (MP).
(66) *tislam īdak* 'May God bless your hand' (thanking for preparing food or any other act performed by hand)'.

God's protection is usually sought as a "good bye":

(67) (a) *a'dar a'ūl ma'a s-salāma?* 'May I take leave now?' [lit. may I say "stay with peace!"?].
(b) *aḷḷāh yisallimik ya sitti 'azīza* 'May God keep you sound and healthy, Mrs. Aziza!' (MP).

When asking to convey greetings:

(68) (a) *kawsar bitsallim 'alēk ya ba* 'Kawsar gives you her regards, father!'

(b) *aḷḷāh ysallimik wi yisallimha* 'Thank you!' [lit. 'May God keep you and her sound and healthy!'] (MP).

The formulae with reference to God that serve as compliments usually take the form of exclamations.

(69) *šī li ḷḷāh!* 'Wow!' [lit. 'Something of God's'] (MP).

(70) *fūl nābit? šī aḷḷāh ya mmu ḥāšim* 'Green broad beans? Wow! Umm Ḥāšim!' (MP).

(71) *inta ibn ḥalāl ya ʿarafi wi fīk šī li ḷḷāh* 'You're a decent fellow, ʿarafi. What a man!' (MP).

(72) *aḷḷāh, aḷḷāh! aḥsant ya šēẖ!* [Used to a sheikh reciting the Quran] 'Wonderful, wonderful, o Sheikh!' (MP).

(73) *aḷḷāh, aḷḷāh, kamān* [When applauding a stage performance] 'Go on, go on! Some more!' (MP).

(74) *aḷḷāh ʿala r-rawāyiḥ il-gamīla* 'How sweet [lit. beautiful] are the scents!' (MP).

(75) (a) *duʾ* 'Taste [this]!'
(b) *aḷḷāh aḷḷāh* 'Wonderful! (MP).

On the other hand, the formulae with reference to God can also be used in strategies of polite refusals. For example, *in šāʾ aḷḷāh*, which means 'if God wishes it so', used generally to the effect of 'yes', as in (81) is also one of the most preferable strategies of refusal (Abdel Samad 1990: 235), which is showcased in (82) and (83):

(76) (a) *nāzil?* 'Are you getting off [the bus]?'
(b) *in šāʾ aḷḷāh* 'Yes, I do'.

(77) *in šāʾ aḷḷāh fi aʾrab furṣa* 'God willing [hopefully], at the earliest chance' (FAS).

(78) *marra tanya in šāʾ aḷḷāh* 'Some other time, God willing' (FAS).

In šāʾ aḷḷāh is one of the most common polite formulae in the whole Arab world; in different contexts it can express: wishes, congratulations, condolences, warning, etc. (Piamenta 1979: 206)

(79) (a) *naʿīman* 'Blessing!' [To someone walking out of the bath].
(b*) aḷḷāh yinʿim ʿalēk ʿuʾbāl ḥammām minā* 'May God bestow favours on you! May you bathe at Minā!'[8].
(a) *in šāʾ aḷḷāh gamīʿan* 'May we both!' (MP).

[8] Minā refers to the name of a town in Saudi Arabia visited during the traditional Islamic pilgrimage.

(80) (a) *izzayy il-ḥāl? in šaʾ aḷḷāh tkūn mabsūṭ* 'How are you? Well, I hope you are happy' (MP).
(b) *il-ḥamdu li llāh ahī mašya* 'Yes, pretty well, thank you!' [lit' 'praise God, it is going'] (MP).

Another expression – *yaḷḷa*, a shortening for *ya aḷḷāh/yā aḷḷāh* 'oh, God' usually serves to prompt people to perform a certain action. As a colloquial exclamation, it can have both positive and negative connotations. However, the pragmatic function of *yaḷḷa* is much wider, Piamenta lists the situations, in which it is used:

> When referring to oneself: to speed oneself, to express promptness, or to comply with a situation; when suggesting to someone: to hasten someone, to urge, to propose to do something, to appease, or to deride, or dismiss someone; to express a wish; to say that a performance is hard, functioning as an adverb of manner: 'hardly'; when repeated (Piamenta 1979: 56).

The following examples show the use of *yaḷḷa* with an aim to hasten someone (81) and (82); to make a proposal (83); and to end a phone call (84):
(81) *yaḷḷa* 'Quick!' (MP).
(82) *yaḷḷa bīna* 'Come on!' (MP).
(83) *yaḷḷa niṭlaʿ barra* 'Let's go outside' (MP).
(84) *yaḷḷa ḅāy* 'So bye then' (MP).

Yaḷḷa may also form an imperfect verb with a meaning of agitation (85).
(85) *ma tyaḷḷa* 'Hurry up!' (MP).

In this book, I focus on the expressions used in response to the taboo of death in Egypt. The intention is to see the extent to which the material is formulaic and how it can be explained. The material analysed here will only involve situations where a speaker is confronted with death that directly affects his/her interlocutor, i.e., the interlocutor has experienced the loss of a beloved person. The formulae are analysed in the context of their grammatical structure, communicative functions and pragmatics as well as their role in constructing the discourse. The next chapter will explain the reasons behind the interest in formulae.

3. What is formulaicity?

In her work *Formulaic Language and the Lexicon*, Wray states that "although we have tremendous capacity for grammatical processing, this is not our only, nor even our preferred, way of coping with language input and output" (2002: 10). According to her, the majority of linguistic production is not processed analytically, which is in contradiction to Chomsky's linguistics. Wray cites two very important arguments that, until recently, were the only counterpoint to the opinion that the entire human linguistic production is generated on an ongoing basis. The first was the observation that idioms cannot be analysed in the way proposed by generative grammar, because such an approach is unable to reflect their meaning. The second was the observation that not all generated sentences, assessed by native speakers as grammatically correct, appear with equal frequency in their relevant situations (Wray 2002). As Wray claims, corpus linguistics and research carried out according to its methods revealed the extent to which natural texts are composed of prefabricated elements, rather than constructed from scratch: "Words belong with other words not as an afterthought but at the most fundamental level" (2002: 13). Sinclair postulated "the idiom principle" to be applied at first place when analysing natural texts, while the "open-choice principle" is applied when necessary (1991: 114). This switching can take place many times back and forth in the process of analysis. A feature of formulaic sequences is their close relationship with the social context in which they are acquainted. Therefore, such expressions constitute a separate set in the lexicon, impossible to fully analyse in isolation from the context.

So, what are formulaic strings? Formulaicity is a feature that occurs within a continuum, which means it is impossible to draw a line between formulaic and non-formulaic expressions. Wray (2002) says they are texts such as rhymes and prayers memorised within oral traditions. They usually include greetings, proverbs, riddles, blessings, curses, time-buyers, turn-holders, discourse markers, repetitions, and other stereotyped phrases. Wray proposes the following definition of a formulaic sequence: "a sequence, continuous or discontinuous, of words or other elements, which is, or appears to be, prefabricated: that is, stored and retrieved whole from memory at the time of use, rather than being subject to generation or analysis by the language grammar" (2002: 9).

What particular researchers include in formulaic sequences differs considerably and various nomenclatures can be found in the literature, e.g., such terms are quite common: "minor ritualistic behavior patterns", "interpersonal verbal routines" (Ferguson 1976), "automatic speech" (Hughlings Jackson, 1874), "automatic" or "nonpropositional speech" (Van Lancker Sidtis 2012a).

When identifying formulaic expressions, various factors are taken into account, none of which appear to be conclusive. First of all, the idiomatic character of a given expression, measured solely by the intuition of native speakers of the language, can be distinguished (Wray 2002). Secondly, the frequency aspect is important. It is believed that the frequency with which certain words occur next to each other in the corpus, suggests their mutual relationship (*ibid.*). Van Lancker Sidtis (2012a) created a four-factor model including form, meaning, context, and personal knowledge for identifying formulaicity. For the study of formulaic language in second language of speakers and people with neurogenic language disturbances a protocol called NEFIPSS (Northridge Evaluation of Formulas, Idioms and Proverbs in Social Situations) was designed by Edward Hall in 1995, allowing for identification of formulae. It should be noted here, however, that neurolinguists understand formulaic language in a slightly broader sense: "Formulaic (formerly automatic) speech, comprising over-learned, recited, and/or emotional utterances of various kinds, including counting, speech formulas (salutations and conversational fillers), swearing, nursery rhymes, familiar lyrics and familiar songs, and all other such expressions known by native speakers" (Van Lancker Sidtis 2012a: 351). Some linguistic elements are seen as formulaic from clinical perspective: swear words, pause fillers ("uh", "um"), interjections, discourse markers such as "well", "so", whereas they are not necessarily all treated this way by linguists.

A result of neurolinguistic work, with patients with mild expressive aphasia and those with fluent aphasia but poor comprehension, in particular, is the "dual process model of language competence" (Van Lancker Sidtis 2012a, Wray and Perkins 2000). As Van Lancker Sidtis remarks: "Observations in clinical adult subjects lead to a profile of cerebral function underlying production of novel and formulaic language, known as the dual processing model. Whereas the left hemisphere modulates newly created language, production of formulaic language is dependent on a right hemisphere/subcortical circuit" (2012b). Brain damage has a different influence on the maintenance of linguistic competence in novel and formulaic language. Patients with lesions within the right hemisphere, especially in the subcortical areas, retained a smaller proportion of formulaic language (Sidtis et al. 2009). On the other hand, patients with lesions in left-hemispheric areas can very often fluently produce polite formulae, various kinds of discourse markers, conventionalised interjections, some serial speech (counting from 1 to 10, days of the week), swear words, nursery rhymes, and verbal routines. Another important fact is that these expressions have their natural articulation and prosody preserved (Sidtis et al. 2009). These patients, however, cannot produce any novel language or have impaired ability to do so. On this basis, it was concluded that formulaic language involves the activity of different areas of the brain than novel language – the areas that are responsible not for analytical abilities, but for direct response to stimuli. Various studies indicate areas of the brain such as the right hemisphere, subcortical circuit, and basal ganglia. On the other hand, when it comes to the exact location of novel language, Van Lancker Sidtis exhausts the topic by saying:

> production of novel utterances engages left-sided cortical areas of the brain including the inferior frontal gyrus (Broca's area), sensorimotor strip, and supplementary motor area via the neural pathways (...), aroused by the reticular formation and the aqueductal grey matter in the brainstem, exchanging commands via the pyramidal and extrapyramidal tracts to the peripheral nervous system (cranial and spinal nerves). Auditory monitoring is enabled by the superior temporal gyrus. Complex motor gestures are executed and monitored by the basal ganglia with participation by the limbic system, which modulates emotion. Integration of motor speech gestures is aided by the thalamus and the cerebellum, especially the right cerebellum. Integration of cortical and subcortical systems, coordinating cognitive and affective streams of information, characterizes all communicative performance (Panksepp, 2003). Damage to any of these structures may interfere with production of spontaneous, novel language (2012a: 351).

According to estimates, the average language user knows between 200,000 and 500,000 formulaic expressions, which explains the complexity of the linguistic forms preserved in people with left hemispheric aphasia (Van Lancker Sidtis 2012a). Speech examples taken from patients with aphasia of the left hemisphere can tell us more precisely what kind of language is formulaic and which is not (Sidtis et al. 2009).

Experimental studies also confirm the dual processing model: "In humans, formulaic and emotional vocalizations occurred when subcortical sites were electrically stimulated during stereotaxic surgical techniques, usually for treatment of epilepsy" (Van Lancker Sidtis 2012a: 355).

The differences between novel and formulaic language are greatly influenced by the different ways in which they are acquired, stored and processed. Many researchers also point to another phenomenon related to damage within the right hemisphere – these patients have a problem with understanding the relationship between utterances and their social context (Van Lancker Sidtis 2012a). In addition, right-hemispheric language is associated with gestures – it turns out that the brain interprets formulaic expressions similarly to gestures. They are often learnt together in a ritualistic manner. This is illustrated by the example of a patient who underwent left hemispherectomy due to brain cancer. Despite his deep aphasia, he could produce some well-articulated expletives, pause fillers, and sentence stems ("I can't", "that's a"). They were accompanied by proper gestures, including sighing and laughing, with no pragmatic deviation from the correct model (Van Lancker Sidtis 2012a: 352). Basal ganglia were recently recognised as the mediators of certain functions such as "initiation, execution, and monitoring of human speech and language" (*ibid.*). Van Lancker Sidtis also notes the similarity between formulaic utterances and animal calls, usually used for warnings and to perform various social functions. The author assumes that certain types of utterances mediated by the limbic system (like swearing and interjections) could have had similar functions in the past, for example they were supposed to scare the enemy away. She adds:

> while human language is cortically represented, animal vocalizations can be elicited only by stimulation of subcortical nuclei (Jürgens 2002). Some scholars have proposed that subcortical structures, which are evolutionarily "old," have also (in addition to cortical lobes) been highly elaborated in the human (Lieberman, 2002). In this view, routinized vocal behaviors occur as species-specific vocalizations in nonhuman mammals, and survive in humans as emotional and formulaic vocalizations. Either alongside the emotional systems or arising out of them, depending on one's viewpoint, are combinatorial systems, seen only in humans and modulated by left hemisphere cortical mechanisms (2012a: 356).

It has now become possible to clarify the subject of this study. The formulaicity of the expressions used as reaction to the taboo of death will be of interest here. In the first place, formulae as such will be analysed, reflecting both the way death is announced as well as condolences and responses to them. Among this group of material, we will encounter a plethora of repetitive expressions. High frequency is one of the factors taken into account in assessing whether a given fragment of text is formulaic or not. Thus, the formulae will be the main focus of this work. In their case, we will also be interested in assessing the extent to which they have a rigid structure and to what degree they are subject to various kinds of formal changes.

4. Material

The material studied in this work consists of examples that illustrate the linguistic response to the taboo of death: death announcements and responses to them in the form of comments offering "condolences". The word "condolences" is written here in quotation marks, because the reaction in response to death announcements in the Arab world is complex in terms of content and does not limit itself to expressions of sympathy and joining the other person in pain.

The material was obtained from Facebook and consists of written utterances. All speakers[9] were adults. No age criterion was adopted, but it can be assumed that the majority of the utterances were made by young people. Another assumption, also unverified, is that the speakers are people with a higher level of education. The snowball method of accessing participants was used, often resulting in speakers with a similar social profile. Some of the speakers, especially when it comes to the authors of death announcements, are my personal Facebook friends. They are people with higher education in humanities or medicine, aged 30–40, professionally related to academic activity or playing an active role in the life of the community, e.g., as charity activists. However, their class affiliation varies, some come from the country's political and financial elite, while others, thanks to hard work and personal talent, have risen from the working class. They addressed their posts to their Facebook friends (judging by the privacy settings), so they could access a maximum of about 500–1,000 people on average (based on the author's number of Facebook friends). An assumption can be made that at least some of those who commented on the posts were people with a similar social profile. The total number of speakers was 774, including 156 men and 618 women. The disproportion in gender was not intended. Post and their comments were randomly selected from the enormous amount of material available.

9 The term "speaker" is used in this work with reference to "the author of the utterance".

In all the examples, the criterion of informality was met. In the study, utterances containing information about the death of a beloved person or a friend as well as reactions to those announcements were analysed. All utterances were personal and no public posts and information about the death of public figures were examined. This is an important condition in the light of the previously discussed dependencies between the tabooisation of death and personal experience. In the studied material, the speaker announces the death of a loved one or addresses the person suffering from the loss. An important element of the situation are the emotions of the person who suffered the loss, as well as the speaker who has to deal with the fragile topic by maintaining an appropriate level of sensitivity and respect for the recipient's feelings.

The material consists of 1,108 utterances, including 20 death announcements, 857 individual comments in response to them, and 220 turns of dialogues. Utterances vary in length, from one-word to multi-sentence elaborations. The entire studied corpus consists of 12,385 words. As for the content, the utterances always refer to the death of the speakers' beloved ones. The deceased are family members or friends of the authors of the posts. They include the elderly relatives (grandmother, parents, aunts and uncles) as well as young people (friends, children). In most cases, additional circumstances deepened the tragedy (for example in the case of the deceased child or when the death was preceded by a long illness). One case in the material stands out – of a young woman who died, as many comments stated, "out of grief", due to the separation from her children kidnapped by her ex-spouse. This woman, in the course of more than a year of being deprived from seeing her kids, developed severe depression. Her death was the result of a stroke she suffered while sleeping. In this case, condolences are also accompanied by curses against her ex-husband.

Since the material was obtained from a social network – Facebook, it has numerous limitations when it comes to its utility in this type of research. This problem will be further discussed below. The main issues include the fact that we do not know much about the relations between the speakers. We cannot tell how close to each other they are or if they are family members or friends. There is a consensus in the Egyptian community that condolences between loved ones take more elaborate forms; more effort is put into comforting the suffering person, not necessarily qualitatively, but quantitatively. As Egyptians put it: "We just talk a lot". A single phrase in such a situation would be considered tactless. Knowing that, we do not have tools to study this type of dependencies using the current material.

Most of the material comes from 2020 and 2021. Additionally, one source of examples (but not of the structural or quantitative analysis) is the material I used in my unpublished doctoral dissertation.

4.1. Language

It is important to locate the discussed material on the sociolinguistic map of Egypt. Specifically, the phenomenon of diglossia, a situation in which two language varieties are used in various contexts of daily life, needs to be explored. The situation of diglossia in a speech community was first described by Ferguson (1959) who defined it as a coexistence of two different language varieties called H (high) and L (low), which function to some extent in a complementary distribution. The prestigious H is used in formal situations such as: political speech, print media, television (information programs), literature, science, etc. The L (dialect, colloquial) is a medium of everyday spoken and written, e.g., in the Internet interactions. However, despite this convenient dichotomy, there are different views about the linguistic situation in Egypt. Many contemporary researchers believe that it should be discussed in terms of a continuum. According to some scholars, on the scale stretching from MSA to EA there are many different varieties of Arabic, e.g., Badawi (1973) suggests there are as many as five. It is true that there are hardly any examples of "pure" EA or MSA usage. Moreover, currently, the linguistic situation is additionally complicated by the strong position of English as a means of instruction in highly prestigious private schools and universities. The language used by interactants in the material studied here is mostly Egyptian Arabic. This, however, requires clarification, as the formulae are, in a way, a link between Classical Arabic and dialect. Most of the formulae, with only a few exceptions, are of classical origin. At the same time, they are expressions commonly known and used in the life of the community, while their pronunciation is often dialectal or dialectalised, e.g. simplified classical. Often, there are two or more possible phonetic renditions of a formula. Additionally, the same formulae are pronounced in different ways depending on the circumstances, e.g. in oral communication the dialectal form may be used, but the classical phonology will be preserved when the formula is a part of a prayer.

Probably in computer-mediated communication (CMC) the use of Classical Arabic and/or Modern Standard Arabic (MSA) is much more frequent than it is in everyday communication, due to the fact that CA provides the patterns for the formulaic expressions with reference to God that form a great part of the etiquette in Egyptian online communication. MSA and CA refine linguistic output by allowing reference to religion and religious culture; they mediate the experience and create distance, especially when the subject of conversation is a highly tabooed one, while also embellishing the utterance and making it more solemn. In conventional forms, a middle variety (between EA and MSA/CA) is used to a greater or lesser extent. Frequent use of MSA/CA may be related to one of the functions of online activity in general: self-presentation and to the fact of language being a tool for constructing identity. Also, in the language of the Internet, in the context of taboo-related topics, more sophisticated formulae might be used, which is facilitated by readymade patterns available through search engines. This is probably culturally conditioned and springs from Arabs' tendency to exuberance in speech (based on authorial reflections on the topic).

As far as the method of typing is concerned (all of the studied texts were written), the Arabic alphabet was used predominantly with some examples of what Egyptians call Franco (or Franco-Arabe), a system based on Roman script with the use of digits to refer to a group of sounds typical for Arabic. The paucity of non-verbal components of communication was to some extent levelled by the use of emoticons, which are, however, not the subject of this study. Emoticons were significant as far as they sometimes expressed some emotional content contradicting the explicit one, and therefore, allowed for the recognition of irony, sarcasm or humour. They were, however, extremely rare in the studied material, probably due to the seriousness of the subject.

4.2. Computer-Mediated Communication

Below I will explain the reasons why I decided to use the online material in this study. Since the emergence of the Internet, there has been a rapid development in new forms of communication related to ever-newer technologies, which have an impact on the language use. Social networking platforms are a relatively new form of contact on the Internet (in Egypt since 2007) but they have created a great deal of space for communication (posts, comments, etc.), which currently occupies a considerable portion of young people's time. Features of online communication include a certain amount of disrespect for the linguistic rules, as well as a greater emphasis on positive content (positive politeness bias) reflected, for instance, in the avoidance of negative statements (taboo – induced elimination). Prensky explains why it might be useful to examine this particular type of communication, for he regards it as the language of a new generation of "digital natives" (2001: 2).

People in the early 21st century spend a huge amount of their time online. It can be assumed that a long exposure to the content and form of online exchanges have and will have an increasing impact on their everyday communication. It results in brevity, hypertextuality and the parallelism of information. This would appear to be a sufficient reason to believe that such a problem is worthy of the discussion. The language used on Facebook is the written form of the Egyptian dialect of Arabic (EA) but, as it will be demonstrated, it has many of the characteristics of spoken language. This type of communication combines the features of the oral and written varieties, due to the fact that the messages posted via social media do not have a clearly defined time of receipt, the writer does not know whether the recipient is connected to the Internet at the time of posting, so they must use communicative strategies corresponding to both forms – the written one (assuming that the recipient receives the message with a delay) and oral (because there is a strong possibility that the message will be read immediately after publication). Sometimes the conversation is carried out almost in real-time and other times it stretches over time, which gives the authors the opportunity to rethink their choice of communicative strategies.

Crystal (2001) assessed CMC data based on seven criteria and decided, there are different types of texts in CMC displaying features of both varieties. Collot and Belmore (1996), as quoted by Dorleijn (2016), applied Biber's (1988) model of written versus oral communication based on six dimensions to the study of CMC data. The examined dimensions were: involved vs. informational production, explicit vs. situation dependent reference, abstract vs. non-abstract information, narrative vs. non-narrative, overt expression of persuasion and on-line informational elaboration. They found out that there were no extremes in most dimensions, which is to say that this communication should probably be located somewhere in between the two varieties discussed earlier. An important feature of CMC is that people generally pay great attention to the form of the utterance posted online, not only in terms of its semantic content. The issue is even more complex; it is crucial to remember that in the case of online posts, the number of potential readers is virtually infinite, particularly while taking into account the timespan and the durability of online posts. This results in a number of techniques applied to make the utterance more attractive, e.g. the use of foreign language, various methods of script (Arabic, Latin, combined Latin with digits) or emoticons. The most challenging problem, however, was how to assess the importance of the "third party factor". Given that the Internet serves self-presentation and self-creation, we must not forget that all of the conversations studied here were easily accessible to a stranger of whose presence the participants in the communicative act must have been aware at the moment of posting the exchange. Therefore, there is an assumption that their decision might have been to choose less risky strategies in most of the taboo-related situations than they would have done if the exchange had been carried out in private. The author of the post, while directing it to the intended recipient or sometimes a group, must assume that some undefined third party might receive it as well as the addressee. Constant awareness of this silent public might affect the way the author forms his/her utterance according to the requirements of their self-image. There is also the possibility that in some cases, this silent public is the actual recipient of the message. Therefore, the high level of control over linguistic production might result in some disturbances when it comes to its authenticity.

In terms of the formulaicity of the utterances, the immediate difficulty for this particular work is the fact that its level may be overstated due to the ease of copying and pasting material while communicating on the Internet.

Moreover, some of the advantages of CMC data discussed by researchers (Dorleijn 2016), namely the fact that written data save time spent on transcription and prevent misunderstanding do not apply to Arabic. In the case of Arabic, the data still must be transcribed due to the multiplicity of spelling systems applied (particularly in mixed CA/MSA – EA varieties). Also, because of the fact that dialects do not have a written tradition, there are various problems in interpreting the resulting variants.

There are several reasons, however, to opt for online material. Firstly, it is the availability of written texts which greatly facilitates the examination of the rules of communication and which, due to the fragile area in question, would be inaccessible to the researcher otherwise. Natural everyday conversations undertaking an intimate and difficult topic of close persons' death is almost impossible for a stranger to record. Furthermore, there would be a great risk of the observer's paradox in spontaneous or elicited data gathered this way. The situations studied here inherently raise strong emotions and therefore the utterances must be obtained in a way that does not involve the intervention of the researcher. On the other hand, the data samples must be natural. This is why I have (albeit grudgingly) rejected the resources available from TV/movie scripts and the like.

5. State of research

As previously stated, formulae are specific elements of language that are retrieved whole from the mental lexicon at the moment of speech production. In this sense, a number of proprieties distinguish formulae from words: "wide-ranging intraphrase flexibility", "mandatory affective and attitudinal nuances", "considerable length" (Van Lancker Sidtis 2012a: 358). The last point probably should be further refined on other occasion. Van Lancker Sidtis refers to them with a term "formuleme", which is an item stored in the mental lexicon, a conglomerate of features relating to meaning (social and affective connotations), linguistic form (grammatical, phonetic, prosodic) and pragmatic contingencies (*ibid.*).
The interest of researchers in formulae dates back to the mid-19th century, when the first studies of aphasiac patients revealed that some parts of language remain intact in their case (Wray 2002). Concepts interpreting the fixedness of idioms began to appear, e.g., in Bobrow and Bell's (1973) model idioms are treated similarly to lexemes in memory. According to them, the analysis mechanism is as follows: literal interpretation is attempted first, and if unsuccessful, a switch is made to select an idiom form the lexicon. Further studies (Swinney and Cutler 1979) employing visual classification latencies did not confirm this theory, on the contrary, they revealed that idioms were processed even faster than non-idiomatic material (Wood 2015).

In one of the first reports in the neurolinguistic field, Winner and Gardner (1977) noted that patients with right hemisphere damage showed problems with a picture matching task involving formulaic metaphors. In the late 80s, a neuropsychological protocol defined a new term – pragnosia (Nelson et al. 1989), a deficit in the social use of language in persons with right hemisphere damage:

> In persons who have sustained right hemisphere damage, many of the elements belonging to the pragmatics of language are deficient: maintaining topic and theme, conversational turn-taking, recognizing when speaker's meaning overrides linguistic meaning in utterances (e.g., in indirect requests, sarcasm, idiomatic expressions), processing humour,

> and appropriately using social expression. When recalling that certain of the natural properties of formulaic language pertain to their appropriate use in social context, it follows that the right hemisphere, so adept at the pragmatic component of language, would play a major role in use of formulas (Van Lancker Sidtis 2012a: 70).

Earlier in 1979, Coulmas published his prominent *Sociolinguistic relevance of routine formulae*. Among other things, he refers to the occurrence profile of formulemes. He notices that some of them are closely related to the particular situation of use, while others are polyfunctional. Also, the obligatoriness of their occurrence is not invariant, and we can distinguish among them ones that are highly, semi- and non-institutionalised in terms of context (Coulmas 1979). He says: "Their obligatoriness serves a very important social function: the more obligatory a formula is, the more it is something like a password giving access to the group where it is habitually employed in some particular situation. The misuse of, or failure to use, an obligatory formula is very revealing, while the correct usage helps to establish the user's membership of a group" (Coulmas 1979: 252). On this basis, it can be concluded that the use of formulae in certain situations constitutes an unmarked choice.

At that time, the problem of formulaicity in language yielded a slightly more serious interest. A few years later, Pawley and Syder's work (1983) on native-like selection and native-like fluency appeared, which allowed to better appreciate the role of formulae in the language competence of users. A few works of Wray were of particular importance to the fields, on functions of formulaic language (2000), where the author proposes an integrative model, which will be a source of explanation for the current work; on the relation between formulaic language and the lexicon (2002) – on formulaicity, and finally, a recapitulation of researchers' knowledge on formulaicity (2012). Another author ought to be mentioned here – Diana van Lancker Sidtis who provides a great deal of insight into formulaicity from the neurolinguistic and clinical perspective, and whose work supports what is known as the dual process model (2012a, 2012b).

5.1. Formulae

There exists a wide variety of expressions classified as formulemes, including sequences remembered for their own sake like rhymes, songs, prayers, quotations (Wray 2002). Their memorisation is accompanied by the acquisition of a specific rhythm facilitating their recall (*ibid.*). Although formulaic language is highly recurrent to the extent that some formulemes undergo idiomatisation and standardisation (Coulmas 1979), Wray notes: "formulaic sequences are a dynamic solution

(...) there is not simply a single stock of formulaic sequences which all speakers first learn, and then draw upon, but rather that the store is constantly changing, to meet the changing needs of the speaker" (2002: 101). Also, excerpts of various texts belonging to individual idiolects: quotations from literature, poems vary significantly, as they reflect personal experience of speakers. Other expressions include politeness formulae. In their case, the referential meaning is highly reduced for the sake of their pragmatic application, "the use is often almost automatic on the proper occasion" (Ferguson 1997a: 215).

Formulae are always an integral part of a given culture. As suggested by Coulmas the investigation of the whole set of formulemes used in a specific community "should reveal interesting characteristics of the respective society, its institutions, habits, customs, norms, and values" (1979: 253). In some cultures recurrent social situations automatically trigger the response in the forms of prefabricated linguistic items (Coulmas 1979), while in others they go unnoticed, e.g., after having their hair freshly washed or after a haircut Egyptians use a formula: *naʿīman* 'blessing' with a response *aḷḷah yinʿim ʿalēk* 'God bless you'. In other cultures, one might simply not say anything, as this is not a remarkable situation in any way. Many factors are taken into account while deciding about the appropriate formula to use, such as time, place, sex, age, familiarity, rank, role relationship, social occasion (Coulmas 1979, Wray 2002). Also, the extent to which formulae are appreciated varies from society to society. Coulmas notices that "attitudes towards prefabricated expressions correlate with the values attributed to originality, flexibility, and individuality" (1979: 261). This view could probably be broadened with a reference to the concept of originality in Arabic poetry; this is not, however, the place for it. One dialogue from the material studied illustrates how blessing is more welcome as a reaction to information about a friend's illness than advice:

(86) (a) *ana taʿabāna ʾawi* 'I am very ill'.
(b) *išrabi mayya ʾabl matnāmi wi kulli ḥāga hatkūn tamām* 'Drink water before going to sleep and everything will be alright'.
(c) *baršamtēn taḥt il-lisān ʾabl in-nōm* 'Two pills under the tongue before going to bed'.
(d) *alf samāla ʿalēki* '[A thousand] health be upon you'.
(a) *aḷḷāh yisallimik ya zuʾ, miš zayy in-nās* 'May God give you health, you well-bred, not like the [other] people'.

Counselling is not what is expected when announcing an illness and the following two pieces of advice were considered a mockery: *išrabi mayya ʾabl matnāmi* 'drink water before going to sleep', *baršamtēn taḥt il-lisān ʾabl in-nōm* 'two pills under the tongue before going to bed'. Blessing, on the other hand, was most welcome: *alf samāla ʿalēki* '[a thousand] health upon you', *aḷḷāh yisallimik ya zuʾ, miš zayy in-nās* 'may God give you health, you well-bred, not like the [other] people'.

Another distinguishable feature of formulae is their ubiquity, both in the case of formulaic language as such, i.e., formulemes, and of formulae in the more colloquial sense of the word (politeness or religious formulae). Ferguson (1997a) believes that only our secular view of the world prevents us from seeing how plentiful they are in everyday life exchanges. Omitting them, although it might be a risky business, can reveal to us the true enormity of their significance (*ibid.*). Wray reviewed the available literature in terms of what percentage of speech consists of formulaic language:

> there are vast discrepancies across studies, regarding the proportion of language that is viewed as formulaic. To take just a few examples, Altenberg (1990) states that "roughly 70% of the running words in the London-Lund Corpus form part of recurrent word combinations of some kind" (p. 134), and by 1998 he has increased this estimate to 80% (p. 102). Moon (1998a), on the other hand, estimates that only between 4% and 5% of the Oxford Hector Pilot Corpus of over 18 million words were parts of the FEIs (fixed expressions including idioms) which she was studying. Butler (1997) identifies repeated phrases as 12.5% of the spoken part of his corpus of Spanish (total 10,000 words), 9% and 8.2% of two transcribed interviews (each 14,000 words), and 5% of the written corpus (57,500 words) depending on the threshold applied (2002: 28).

Later on, Wray also points out that not only the sheer number of occurrences plays a role in assessing the importance of formulae in everyday speech. The author draws our attention to the fact that the frequency of, for example, the expression "happy birthday" in the corpus might be less important than the fact that in the case of giving someone a birthday wish, this particular expression is used in about 98% of cases.

Neurolinguistic and linguistic studies indicate that the primary function of formulaicity is probably to reduce the processing load of the speaker's production and the interlocutor's comprehension. However, this way of seeing the problem is far from being exhaustive. Coulmas (1979) quotes Malinowski's (1923) reflections on the function of formulae in the daily life of communities. Above their communicative and phatic functions, there is a socialisation role: they are used to strengthen social bonds. This is consistent with Abdel Samad's (1990) findings about politeness formulae in Egyptian Arabic. According to her the formulae serve to:

- establish friendly relations during an interaction,
- predict the actions of the conversation partner,
- prevent the danger of misunderstanding,
- create closeness or distance,
- get attention,
- start the conversation,
- organise the exchange of thoughts,

- mark objection, surprise, or interest,
- minimise imposition,
- intensify statements,
- mark superficial politeness.

Similar results can be found in (Salomond 1974) on rituals of encounter in Maori society, and formulae serve to:

- regulate emotional situations,
- reduce the complexity of social interaction,
- facilitate decision processes,
- organise reactions to social situation,
- furnish the verbal means for communicating.

According to Aijmer's (1996) "conversational routines" perform socio-interactional functions (thanking, requesting, offering and apologising), indicate an orientation to the content and mark the organisation of the text. Local and global markers refer to the relation between utterances and between elements of the macro-structure respectively. Attitudinal routines mark behaviours and emotions. Another function of routinised formulae is to emphasise the group affiliation of speakers (Wray 2002), by, among others, "indicating the speaker's familiarity with and readiness to conform to the norms of the group" (Coulmas 1979). Wray (2002) draws attention to yet another function of formulae, namely, the manipulation of the interlocutor in order to achieve certain actions on their part or make a certain impression.

In terms of their pragmatics and social functioning formulae vary according to a number of social dimensions, Ferguson (1976: 145) distinguishes:

- length of time elapsed since previous encounter,
- distance between communicators,
- number of individuals in the relevant groups,
- relative social status of the communicators.

Ferguson goes on by saying: "in some human societies the superior initiates the greeting (e.g. Moroccan Arabic), in others the inferior does so (e.g. Gonja), and in still others the social dominance differentiation is more complex (e.g. American English), but what is universal is the correlation between structure of formula and the social (or sociotemporal, sociospatial) dimension" (1976: 145). The author (*ibid.*) enumerates three important diachronic features of polite formulae:

- weakening (aphesis, contraction, erosion), related to the fact that they lack referential meaning, as an example he quotes the weakening from "How are you?" to "Hi!" in American English;
- archaism – due to their affinity with memorized texts such as nursery rhymes, they tend to retain archaic forms;

- areal diffusion – a tendency of those elements of language to spread along with other elements of culture (e.g. Arabic greetings spreading along with Islam to non-Arab speech communities).

Wray makes a very interesting observation on the formulaic expression:

> is subject to detachment from the effects of the live grammar and lexicon. The string is no longer obliged to be grammatically regular or semantically logical. Sequences become frozen, or fossilized, and as a result often retain words or grammatical forms which are no longer current in the language. For example, *if I were you* contains the subjunctive form of *be*, and *by dint of* features an obsolete lexical item. The meaning may also become detached from the literal. Thus, the two formulae *I couldn't care less* and *I could care less* mean the same thing, even though they appear to be opposites (2002: 33).

As for the meaning of formulae, it is linked by a number of relations – on the one hand, with the grammatical form and, on the other, with the context of use. Furthermore, the meaning cannot be separated from the grammatical form of a word (Wray 2002). Coulmas sees the meaning of formulae as "conditioned by the behavior patterns of which they are an integrated part" (1979: 241).

5.2. Research on formulae in Arabic

The corpus of pragmatic work on Arabic formulae is rather limited. It includes, for example, Ali El-Sayed's study of politeness formulae in English and Arabic (1990). Lancioni (2009) presented a very interesting work on formulaicity in Arabic, which, unfortunately for the current study, focuses on poetry. Ayman Nazzal examined the pragmatic functions of the recitation of Quranic verses with special attention to *in šāʾ aḷḷāh* 'God willing' (2010). There are also a few works focused on specific issues which include Maan Muhammed Aubed's study of polite requests in English and Arabic (2012), Baidaa' F. Noori's analysis of polite formulae in English and Arabic (2012). Studies on Arabic dialects other than Egyptian include the Yemeni dialect, e.g., Al-Marrani and Binti Sazalie's study of polite requests strategies by Yemeni Females (2010a) and their work on the same issue in Yemeni female–male interactions (2010b). When it comes to terms of address there are a few works on dialects other than Egyptian, e.g., Yassin's (1977a, 1977b, 1978) on Kuwaiti. There are also a number of contrastive studies, for instance, Rula Fahmi Bataineh's work on congratulating, thanking and apologising in Jordanian Arabic and American English (2013). Said Hassan Farahat examined the politeness phenomena in Palestinian Arabic and Australian English (2009). Hanaa Ali Al-Qahtani's contrastive study between spoken Saudi Arabic and spoken British English focuses on female use of politeness in the act of offering (2009). Ebaa Yahya studied condolences in Iraqi Arabic with reference to English (2010). Some papers are specifically concerned with translation, for example Bahaa-Eddin M. Mazid's study of politeness formulae in Emirati Arabic (2006). Badarneh (2020) studied formulaic expressions of politeness in Jordanian Arabic and Abdou conducted research on the semantic structure of Arabic idioms (2010).

In terms of work on formulae used in the discourse about death, there were a few attempts to analyse obituaries and condolences, e.g. Al-Khatib and Salem in Jordanian and British newspapers (2011), Sawalmeh in Jordanian press (2019), Hidaya and Obeidat (2015/2016) in the Algerian dialect of Arabic. Yasser A. Gomaa and Yeli Shi (2012) analysed death euphemisms in Arabic and Chinese.

The number of papers on formulaicity-related issues in Egyptian Arabic remains small. Some of them include contrastive studies aimed at facilitating language learning and understanding the acquisition of politeness formulae and their usage, and excerpt the rules governing the choice of strategies for language learners who do "face threatening acts"[10]. Fatma Abdel Samad (1990) examined a broad notion of politeness strategies in spoken British English and Egyptian, in which she discussed a certain number of formulae. Another scholar – Amany Abd El-Moneen El Shazly (1994) dealt with requesting strategies in American English and Egyptian Arabic, as well as English spoken by Egyptian learners of this language. The act of refusal in Egyptian Arabic as executed by American learners was examined by Nader Morkus (2014). The author compared the performance of the learners to that of native speakers in order to investigate the relation between the learner's language proficiency and their pragmatic competence. The study also examined the structure of refusals on the level of discourse. Amira Elserafy and Saliha Arseven (2013) investigated politeness, directness and honorifics in Egyptian Arabic and Turkish requests. They examined the language of young people pursuing their higher education by means of a DCT (discourse-completion task) that consisted of ten written situations with different levels of "social power" and "imposition". According to them, conventional indirectness was the most prevailing strategy used by both the Egyptians and the Turks. However, Egyptian students showed significantly more preference for directness and non-conventional indirectness. Beside these contrastive studies there have been a number of other papers investigating issues of politeness in Egyptian Arabic. Rachel Marian Harris (1984) studied the conversation in EA examining the issue of truth in the context of politeness. Also, a work by David Wilmsen, *Understatement, Euphemism, and Circumlocution*

[10] Face threatening act (en. FTA) – a term used in Brown and Levinson's theory of politeness (1987) to describe situations when speaker's or hearer's self images are put at threat as a result of the tensions in the act of communication.

in Egyptian Arabic Cooperation in Conversational Dissembling (2010) is worth mentioning here.

However, the most important for this study, and worth highlighting are four of the Ferguson's articles concerning formulae in Syrian Arabic: "God wishes in Syrian Arabic" (1997a), "The blessing Lord be upon you" (1997c), "The Structure and Use of Politeness Formulas" (1976) and "Root-Echo Response in Syrian Arabic" (1997b) and Devin Stewart's articles on paronomastic responses to curses and blessings (1996, 1997, 2014). Ferguson in his work, "The Structure and Use of Politeness Formulas", (1976) deals with the topic of lexical and grammatical dependences at a level higher than that of sentence concerning formulae. He analyses, among other things, root-echo responses to Syrian Arabic politeness formulae. These are used in response to each formula that according to Ferguson (1997b: 200) "(a) has no specific paired response, and (b) contains a word built on the particular root of the verb in the response." As an example he gives an expression *aḷḷāh yibārik fīk* 'God bless you' as an appropriate response to any formula without a specific obligatory response and containing the root B-R-K. Devin Stewart's "Root-echo Responses in Egyptian Arabic Politeness Formulae" (1996) and "Impoliteness Formulae: The Cognate Curse in Egyptian Arabic" (1997), as well his work on Morrocan Arabic (2014) are an excellent source of formulae along with their interpretation, specifically on the paronomastic type. According to Stewart, root-echo responses are politeness formulae that employ a cognate of a verb or noun used by an interlocutor during an initial phrase. They represent a magical element of language: "By using the cognate, one seizes on a relic of the interlocutor's speech. Reframing this relic in a context invoking the supernatural represents a doubly effective use of the magic power of language. It is obvious that paronomasia and especially the use of cognates are important rhetorical devices in Arabic and the Semitic languages" (Stewart 1996: 171). The function of paronomastic responses is to confirm the message and strengthen the power of the blessing: "The key element in the exchange is the repetition of the root letters, which serves to confirm an expression of politeness through the invocation of the higher plan of the divine or supernatural" (Stewart 1996: 173). Using them, as in the case of other types of blessing, is based on a reference to a supernatural agency. The following summary briefly presents Stewart's (1996: 163–173) findings on root-echo responses in blessings:

- The root-echo response consists of an optative verb either in the perfect or (most commonly) imperfect tense;
- If the optative verb is perfect, it precedes the subject (*naʿam aḷḷāh ʿalēk, ḥannāk aḷḷāh*);
- If the optative verb is imperfect, it follows the subject (*aḷḷāh yinʿim ʿalēk, aḷḷāh yiḥannīk*);
- Most of the optative verbs are affirmative; however, the negative might also occur;

- The verb is a cognate of the key word in the formula (verb or noun);
- If the cognate word in the response is a noun, another verb is introduced as the optative;
- It is possible to omit the subject, which depends on the verb; certain verbs must have God as a subject;
- Most of the responses are fixed expressions and are used automatically;
- Women use root-echo responses much more often and are more likely to produce innovative forms;
- In blessings, the repetition of root letters, unlike in curses, must be exact and not distorted;
- The responses are semantically nonsense when interpreted in isolation from their initial utterances;
- The initiator might not be stated explicitly; the response might be a reaction to someone's laughter or smile (Ḍ-Ḥ-K), the act of kissing (B-W-S), etc.

Examples of such blessing found in Stewart's article (1996) include:
(87) *furṣa saʿīda* 'a fortunate opportunity' (functionally equivalent to 'it's been nice to meet you') > *ana asʿad* 'I am more fortunate' (DS).
(88) *minawwar* 'You are lighting up' (for example our house, said by a host to a guest to convey the meaning 'it's so nice to have you here') > *bi nūrak* 'with your light' (DS).
(89) *mabrūk* 'congratulations' > *aḷḷāh yibārik fīk* 'May God bless you' (DS).
(90) *maʿa s-salāma* 'good-bye' (literally, 'with peace, or safety') > *aḷḷāh yisallimak* 'May God keep you safe' (DS).
(91) *naʿīman* 'May you feel comfortable' (said as a compliment to one who has just taken a bath, shaved, or had a haircut) > *aḷḷāh yinʿim ʿalēk* 'God bless you' (DS).
(92) *šarraftuna* 'You've honoured us' (formula of a leave-taking uttered by the host to his guests) > *aḷḷāh yišarraf miqdārak* 'May God enhance your position' (DS).
(93) *ṣabāḥ il-ḫēr* 'Good morning' > *yisʿid ṣabāḥak* 'God make your morning happy' (DS).
(94) *bi ṣiḥḥa wi ʿafya* 'May it give you health and strength' (said to one eating or drinking) > *ʿafākum aḷḷāh* 'May God grant you strength' (DS).

Among other important works are M. Piamenta's brilliant *Islam in Everyday Arabic Speech* (1979) is an invaluable source of examples. Two non-linguistic works were crucial for the current study too: Sania Hamady's *Temperament and Character of the Arabs* (1960) and Raphael Patai's *The Arab Mind* (1973). All of the above provide a deep insight into Arabic, or, specifically, Egyptian culture and language, and present a valuable source of information.

6. Structural notes

The current quantitative analysis encompasses 857 comments made in reaction to death announcements, the vast majority of which consist in condolences and blessings expressed with a set of conventional formulae. Single-formula expressions were very rare, most often at least a few of the elements presented below were represented. The scheme shown in the table below accounts for most of the typical formulae and the standard order in which they appear in the material studied. Additionally, the table shows the percentage of a given slot's occurrence in the material studied.

Table 1. The structure of condolences

Opening formula	Framing formula		CORE				Supplement				Framing formula	Closing formula
General reference to God 10.3%	Death-related expression 11.7%	DM	Supplication 1 73.4%	DM	Supplication 2 43,9%	DM	Blessing for the deceased 43%	DM	Blessing for the mourner 24,1%	DM	Death-related expression 1,4%	General reference to God 0,5%

The most typical example of a reaction to a death announcement has a multi-stage structure. Each of the stages is optional, yet the core appears in a majority of cases. Between the stages, the table shows empty slots called here discourse markers (DM). They can be filled with invocations directed at God (vocative forms), terms of address, terms of endearment or elements confirming blessings, e.g., *amīn* 'amen'.

The core of condolences is usually two-cola, consisting of two twin supplications – requesting mercy and forgiveness for the deceased. Most frequently, they have the form of an optative expressed with the imperfective verb or, less frequently, imperative with vocative forms addressed directly to God. Perfect tense occurs as well, although it is rare. An explicitly expressed subject appears only with the first element of the group, while the second one is introduced with the *wa*/*wi*[11] conjunction. Elements of the core might be separated by DM slots or appear one after another joined with the *wa*/*wi* conjunction.

(95) *aḷḷāh yirḥamu wi yiġfirlu* 'May God have mercy on him and forgive him'.

(96) *ya rabb irḥamha wi ġfirlaha* 'Oh, Lord, have mercy on her and forgive her'.

The stage which appears directly after the core is the supplement, i.e., an additional group of formulae, usually two-cola as well but with common diversions from the rule. The first part is a blessing for the deceased, in which the writer asks God to grant the deceased a place in heaven. The second part is a blessing for the mourner – the author requests relief, peace and patience (*ṣabr*) for the suffering bereaved one. It happens that only one of the formulae is used, while in certain cases more developed supplements occur as well. Optional DMs occur between the two elements of the supplement.

Opening and framing formulae as well as closing/framing formulae are complementary expressions which provide a framework for the whole utterance, occurring at the beginning or at the end. An opening/closing formula is usually a general invocation to God expressing his almightiness, while a framing formula is an expression which refers to the situation of death in particular. Both are common in the whole Arab Islamic world, not limited to Egypt.

The material studied includes occurrences of utterances considerably restricted in form (e.g. *al-baqā' li llāh* 'only God is eternal'), unconventional ones, or expressions which are not condolences or blessings but reactions to death of a different type. Such examples will be accounted for at the end this chapter. All the slots and their contents are discussed in more detail below.

6.1. Opening formula > General reference to God

This occurs 88 times, which means the slot is filled in 10.3% of the 857 comments. It encompasses three formulae: *lā ḥawl wa lā quwwa illa bi ḷḷāh* 'there is no power and no strength save in God'[12], also present in an extended version *lā ḥawl wa lā quwwa illa bi ḷḷāhi al-ʿalī al-ʿaẓīm* 'there is no power and no strength save in God, the highest (high), the greatest'; the expression which opens the Islamic oath: *lā*

[11] As it is almost impossible to decide on the variant *wa* (standard)/*wi* (dialectal) used in the material based on written data, I assume that the dialectal EA *wi* (or *u*) is used unless the environment suggest otherwise.

[12] A natural, mixed pronunciation was reflected in the transcription instead of the standard *lā ḥawla wa lā quwwata illā bi llāh*.

ilāha illā ḷḷāh 'there is no deity but God', which once appears as *lā ilāha illā ḷḷāh waḥdu* 'there is no deity but God, he alone'; and *aḷḷāhu akbar* 'God is the greatest'.

Table 2. Opening formula

lā ḥawl wa lā quwwa illa bi ḷḷāh 'There is no power and no strength save in God' (75)	*al-ʿalī l-ʿaẓīm* 'The highest, the greatest' (12)
lā ilāha illā ḷḷāh 'There is no deity but God' (13)	*waḥdu* 'he alone' (1)
aḷḷāhu akbar 'God is the greatest' (3)	

6.2. Framing formula > Death-related expression

This occurs 100 times, which means the slot is filled in 11.7% of the cases. A framing formula is a very general death-related expression recognisable in the whole Arab world. It usually serves as an introduction to condolences, but it can stand alone as well. It is based on two formulae: *al-baqāʾ li llāh* 'only God is eternal' – used by Muslims to confirm their faith in that only God is everlasting and all humans must die, and *inna li ḷḷāh wa inna ilayhi ragiʿūn* 'verily we belong to God, and verily to him do we return'[13], which says that the human life on Earth is only a stage in eternal life and every human returns to God sooner or later.

The first formula is sometimes extended with a repetition of: *al-baqāʾ wi d-dawām li llāh* 'the eternity and perpetuity belong to God' or with *waḥdu* 'he alone' – expression appearing from time to time. The second of the formulae is the (2:156) verse of the Surah Al-Baqara known as "a supplication in times of hardship". It is "recommended" when misfortune or disaster strikes; therefore, it occurs regularly in all the cases studied.

Table 3. Framing formula

al-baqāʾ li llāh 'Only God is eternal' (62)	*waḥdu* 'He alone' (6)
al-baqāʾ wi d-dawām li llāh 'The eternity and perpetuity belong to God' (10)	*waḥdu* 'He alone' (10)
inna li ḷḷāh wa inna ilayhi ragiʿūn 'Verily we belong to God, and verily to him do we return' (28)	

[13] Mixed, dialectalised variant of transcription is used instead of *innā li ḷḷāh wa innā ilayhi rāǧiʿūna*.

In one case, the slot of the framing formula is filled with an expression which can count as formulaic, yet stands out from the whole of the material: *inna li ḷḷāhi mā aḫaḏa wa lahu mā aʿṭā wa kull šay' ʿindahu bi ağlin musammā* 'whatever God takes is for him and whatever he gives, is for him, and everything with him has a limited term'[14]. What is particularly curious, however, is that one of the most common phrases in spoken language, *il-ba'iya fi ḥayātak* 'the rest is in your life'[15], an equivalent of "I am sorry for your loss' occurs only once in the material of this study. Moreover, while such formulae are considered sufficient comments in spoken language, they are only a type of introduction to a multi-formula utterance in the material studied here. This indicates that Internet users exhibit a greater level of control over linguistic production and possibly a more conscious creation of utterances in terms of stylistics. The independent expression of *al-baqā' li llāh* occurred 13 times, while *inna li ḷḷāh wa inna ilayhi ragiʿūn* was used only once, except for when it accompanied *al-baqā' li llāh.* Opening and framing formulae occur in 10.3% and 11.7% of the comments studied respectively. Most commonly, only one of them is used, but when they do occur together, they are not separated by a DM slot. The opening formula slot is always filled by one of the three formulae only, while the framing formula slot might be filled with more than one at a time, the most common being *al-baqā' li llāh* followed by *inna li ḷḷāh wa inna ilayhi ragiʿūn.*

6.3. Core

The core of condolences is usually a two-cola set of supplications for divine mercy and forgiveness for the deceased. The second formula generally repeats the meaning of the one, introducing a semantic nuance or a specification. There are rare cases of cores including more than two elements, consisting in a succession of supplications of similar meaning, often linguistically sophisticated. Furthermore, every added formula increases the probability of standard realisation of spelling and pronunciation, as formulae used in this manner are most commonly derived from the classical language, e.g., from the Quran.

(97) *yigmaʿkum ʿala ḫēr ʿandu fi d-daragāt il-ʿula min il-ganna bi giwār sayyidna muḥammad il-muḫtār ṣalla aḷḷāh ʿalēh wa yigmaʿna bīh fi ğannātin wa nahr wa miqʿad ṣidqin malīkin muqtadir* 'May he unite you in the highest place in heaven in the neighbourhood of Muhammad, the chosen one, peace be

[14] Translation by M. Muhsin Khan for *Sahih Bukhari Book*: 23, Hadith: 1284, https://sunnah.com/bukhari, access: July 2021.

[15] It is understood as: "you are the survivor, and the deceased's extension".

upon him, and unite us with him "in the midst of gardens and rivers in an assembly of truth, in the presence of a sovereign omnipotent""[16].

6.3.1. Core I

In a vast majority of cases, the first element of the core is based on the root of R-Ḥ-M, semantically related to the concept of God's mercy. The slot is filled in 73.4% (629 examples) of the material studied, with 590 examples built around the R-Ḥ-M root. The supplications of the first part of the core are most often wishful sentences with predicate expressed as an optative in the form of the imperfect *yirḥam* 'have mercy' (523 examples). The most typical example is *rabbina yirḥamu* 'may Lord have mercy on him'. Most commonly, the subject in this type of sentences is *rabbina* 'our Lord' (323 examples) or *aḷḷāh* 'God' (194 examples). The subject does not need to be expressed explicitly. Sometimes the *ya rabb* vocative expression addressed to God in a DM is placed before the core while sometimes the subject remains purely implied. In a vast majority of cases (488 times), the object is a third-person pronoun corresponding to the deceased person or, much less commonly (35 times), a second-person one. In the latter situation, the speaker applies the stylistic device of directly addressing the deceased. Such examples usually appear when the deceased was also the speaker's relative, not only a relative of the addressee of the comment. Rarely, the object of these sentences can be a term of kinship. Additionally, sentences of this type may be extended with a prepositional phrase (PP) or in the form of *al-mafʿūl al-muṭlaq*[17]. A repetition of the R-Ḥ-M root is characteristic here: *raḥma wāsiʿa* 'great mercy', *bi raḥmatihi* 'with his mercy', *bi raḥmitu al-wasiʿa* 'with his great mercy'.

Table 4. Core I, example 1

aḷḷāh 'God' (194)	*yirḥam* 'have mercy' (523)	3rd (484)	*raḥma wāsiʿa* 'great mercy' (14)
rabbina 'Our Lord' (323)		2nd (35)	*bi raḥmatihi* 'with his mercy' (2)
		kinship term (2)	*bi raḥmitu al-wāsiʿa* 'with his great mercy' (1)

[16] A fragment of Quranic verse Surah Qamar (54: 54–55), *Translation by* A. Yusuf Ali, https://quranyusufali.com, access: July 2021.

[17] *Al-mafʿūl al-muṭlaq* in CA/MSA is a term referring to a cognate object – a verbal noun derived from the same root as the one in the verb. It is used either for emphasis or within a noun phrase with adjectives (indicating, e.g., the manner).

Another type of repetition is the cloning of the predicate, where the speaker, somehow "by the way" asks God for mercy for a deceased on their side and for all the deceased.

(98) *rabbina yirḥamu wi yirḥam bāba* 'May Lord have mercy on him and on dad'.

(99) *rabbina yirḥamu huwwa wi abūya* 'May Lord have mercy on him and on my father'.

(100) *rabbina yirḥamha wi yirḥam mawtāna kulluhum* 'May Lord have mercy on her and (have mercy) in all of our deceased ones'.

It is much less commonly that the R-Ḥ-M root creates a predicate in the imperative form, e.g., *aḷḷāhumma rḥamu* 'oh God, have mercy'. In such a case, the agent role is played by the *aḷḷāhumma* vocative form. There were 15 such cases in the material studied. Several of them had additional adverbials repeating the root of the predicate, as in the previous examples. It is natural in this case for the object to be expressed in the third person exclusively.

Table 5. Core I, example 2

aḷḷāhumma 'Oh, God' (15)	*irḥam* 'have mercy' (15)	3rd (15)	*raḥma was'a* 'great mercy' (2)
			bi raḥmitak il-was'a 'with your great mercy' (1)

Two examples stand out from among the others in the material – one of them is a sentence with the *irḥamha* 'have mercy' imperative which uses *rabbi* 'my Lord', a form of the subject extremely rare in Egypt: *rabbi rḥamha* 'oh Lord, have mercy on her'. The second untypical sentence is *aḷḷāhumma yirḥamha* 'oh Lord, may [he] have mercy on her', where the vocative is followed by an imperfective form instead of an imperative.

The R-Ḥ-M may also appear in the perfective form, which is perceived as more classical and less typical for the Egyptian dialect: *raḥamahu (raḥamhu, raḥamu) aḷḷāh* 'may Lord have mercy on him'. In the studied material 10 such examples were found, in each case with the subject being expressed explicitly in the form of the word *aḷḷāh* 'God'. The word order in the sentences also reflects the classical model – the verbal predicate appears at the beginning, followed by an object in the form of a third-person pronoun (the deceased), the agent only appearing in the third position. Such sentences may be complemented by: *raḥmatan wāsi'a* (or more often *raḥma was'a*) 'great mercy', *fī l-firdaws al-a'lā* (or *il-fardūs il-a'la*) 'the greatest paradise', *huwwa waḥdu* 'only he'.

Table 6. Core I, example 3

raḥam 'Have mercy' (10)	3rd (10)	*aḷḷāh* 'God' (10)	*fi l-firdaws al-aʿlā* 'the greatest paradise' (1)
			huwa waḥdu 'only he' (1)
			raḥma wāsiʿa 'great mercy' (1)

Two examples with the R-Ḥ-M root in a perfective form occur together with nouns of generalising meaning. In those cases, the VSO word order is used:
(101) *raḥam aḷḷāh aṭ-ṭayyibīn* 'May God have mercy on good [people]'.
(102) *raḥam aḷḷāh al-ğamīʿ* 'May God have mercy on everyone'.

Additionally, one example includes the highly formal expression *faqīda* 'deceased':
(103) *raḥam aḷḷāh al-faqīda raḥma wāsiʿa* 'May God have great mercy on the deceased'.

Another root present in core I is Ġ-F-R, much rarer in the material than R-Ḥ-M. Its meaning is related to forgiveness and absolution, so it is semantically related to the former. If the predicate is expressed with an imperfective form (similarly to the case of the verb *yirḥam* 'to have mercy'), a subject is not necessary, yet it is generally present, in a vast majority of cases as *rabbina* 'our Lord'. The object is introduced with a PP with the preposition *li* 'for' and expressed in the form of a third-person pronoun (the deceased person).

Table 7. Core I, example 4

rabbina 'Our Lord' (15)	*yiġfir* 'forgive' (19)	*li* + 3rd (19)
aḷḷāh 'God' (1)		

The predicate in the core I supplication may be the Ġ-F-R root in the imperative form, which will, similarly to the previous examples, occur in sentences beginning with the *aḷḷāhumma* 'Oh, God' vocative. It was only in one example that the vocative was omitted. A PP with a third-person pronoun or with a kinship term constitutes the object.

Table 8. Core I, example 5

aḷḷāhumma 'Oh, God' (16)	*iġfir* 'forgive' (17)	*li* + 3rd (16)
		li + kinship term (1)

The classically ordered examples of the sentences shown here separately are rare cases indeed. They begin with a perfective predicate followed by the subject (*aḷḷāh* 'God') and a third-person object expressed with a PP.

Table 9. Core I, example 6

ġafar 'Forgive' (4)	*aḷḷāh* 'God' (4)	*li* + 3rd (4)

(104) *ġafar aḷḷāh lahā* 'May God forgive her'.

A separate group within core I involves nominal sentences, whose central idea is also expressed with the R-Ḥ-M root, for instance:
(105) *raḥmit aḷḷāh 'alēh* 'God's mercy on her'.

Table 10. Core I, example 7

<table>
<tr><td colspan="2">raḥmit rabbina 'Our Lord's mercy' (1)</td><td rowspan="2">'ala + 3rd 'on' (20)</td></tr>
<tr><td colspan="2">raḥmit aḷḷāh 'God's mercy' (16)</td></tr>
<tr><td>alf raḥma '(A thousand) mercy (19)</td><td>wi nūr 'and light' (9)</td><td>'ala + 2nd 'on' (4)</td></tr>
</table>

The material also includes one example with inverted word order:
(106) *'alēh raḥmit aḷḷāh* 'On her God's mercy'.

God, as the one who grants mercy, is most often referred to as *aḷḷāh*, while the more dialectal *rabbina* 'our Lord' occurs only once. It is in one example that we can observe both forms being used:
(107) *raḥmit rabbina 'alēh, raḥmit aḷḷāh 'alēh* 'Our Lord's mercy on him, God's mercy on him'.

6.3.2. Core II

The second part of the core occurs 376 times, which constitutes 43.9% of the comments analysed. It is based on a supplication to God for the sins of the deceased to be forgiven. Multi-formulaic expressions are relatively common here, yet the most commonly found is a single optative sentence with the verb *ġafar* 'forgive' (298 examples). The function of the optative is most commonly served by an imperfective form (285 examples). A subject expressed explicitly in core I is not repeated here and the whole part is introduced with the *wa/wi* 'and' conjunction. The verb *ġafar* requires an object introduced with a prepositional phrase (PP) with the preposition *li* 'for'. Most often, the object is a third person pronoun referring to the deceased or, less often, a second person pronoun, similarly to core I. The most typical example of core II is, therefore, the following expression:

(108) *wi yiġfirlu* 'And forgive him'.

The verb occurs much more rarely in its imperative form, and as rarely as twice in its perfective form. Additionally, one example (109) was not included in the table below due to its subject being expressed explicitly, which is the only situation of such a kind in the whole material studied.

Table 11. Core II

yiġfir + *li* 'Forgive' (287)	3rd (311)	*gamīʿan* 'every' (1)	*zunūb* 'sins' + 3rd (1)
iġfir + *li* 'Forgive' (11)	2nd (27)		*qadra karamihi wa raḥmatihi wa maġfaratihi wa ʿafwihi* 'with the enormity of your generosity, mercy and forgiveness' (1)
ġafar + *li* 'Forgive' (2)	*gamīʿ al-muslimīn* 'all Muslims' (1)		*winta arḥam ir-raḥimīn* 'you are the most merciful' (1)
yirḥam 'Have mercy' (14)			*bi raḥmitu* 'with his mercy' (1)
irḥam 'Have mercy' (22)			*bi-raḥmitak* 'with your mercy' (1)
raḥam 'Have mercy' (3)			*fi l-ganna wa naʿīmiha* 'in heaven and its bliss' (1)
yuḥsin ilā 'Bestow good upon' (16)			
yaʿfū ʿan 'Pardon' (7)			
ʿafā ʿan 'Forgive' (1)			
yisāmiḥ 'Forgive' (8)			
yatakarram 'Give generously' (1)			
yatagāwaz ʿan 'Forgive one's sins' (1)			

(109) *ġafar aḷḷāh zunūbu* 'May God forgive him his sins'.

There are five further verbs that appear in the core II slot, the most common of them being *yuḥsin* 'bestow good' (16 times) which introduces a pronoun-based object with the *ilā* 'upon' preposition. Two others that reappear are *ya'fu* 'forgive' and *yisāmiḥ* 'forgive', while *yatakarram* 'give generously' and *yatagāwaz* 'forgive one's sins' occur only once. There are, however, three occurrences of the last verb in a slightly altered construction:
(110) *yatagāwaz 'an say'ātu* 'May (God) forgive his sins'.

Most of the sentences filling the slot are conventional expressions realised in line with dialectal phonology, yet the fewer the occurrences, the greater the probability of an expression coming from the standard (to be precise – the classical) language and such is the probable pronunciation. The examples including perfective verbs can certainly be deemed classical, as such a form is not used in the optative function in the Egyptian dialect. This is additionally confirmed by the *ġafar* 'forgive' verb occurring twice with objects in the form of PPs with pronouns in their dual form (referring to two deceased persons).
(111) *wa ġafara lahumā* 'And may (God) forgive the two of them'.

Additionally, the basic supplication in core II may be complemented with praise for God serving a persuasive or propitiatory function, e.g., *winta arḥam ir-raḥimīn* 'you are the most merciful of all'. The expression *qadra karamihi wa raḥmatihi wa maġfaratihi wa 'afwihi* 'the enormity of your generosity, mercy and forgiveness', has a similar function, suggesting that divine generosity and mercy have no boundaries. Moreover, it is not uncommon to extend the request for divine mercy and forgiveness to other deceased persons, particularly relatives of the speaker, as well as onto oneself and other living persons. Additionally, the beneficiary of the blessing may be every deceased Muslim. Such requests occur often in other slots as well and it might be stated that they are formulaic in character:
(112) *rabbina yirḥamu huwwa wa bāba wi yiġfirluhum* 'May Lord have mercy on him and dad, and forgive them'.
(113) *wi yiġfirluhum gamī'an* 'And forgive them all'.
(114) *yirḥamu wi yirḥam waldi wi mawtāna wi mawta l-muslimīn* 'May [he] have mercy my father and our deceased, and all deceased Muslim'.

To sum up, the core is usually a two-part structure. Core I expresses a request for mercy and core II for forgiveness, the contrary being less common. The core is also quite often found in a single-element version, in which case, the vast majority is based on the R-Ḥ-M root. There are cases of a more developed core II, where the request for forgiveness is multi-formulaic, e.g. (115):

(115) *wi yiġfirlaha wi yisāmiḥha* 'And forgive her and pardon her'.

One example stands out among others which occur in core II due to its reference to paradise (*ganna*), which provides a semantic basis for the following slot.

(116) *wi yuḥsin ilayhi fi l-ganna wi na'imha* 'And [may he] bestow good upon him in heaven and its bliss'.

6.4. Supplement

Another section of the comments is dubbed "supplement" here as it almost never occurs alone, but rather complements the supplications expressed in the core. This slot, similarly to the previous one, consists of two elements – blessings. The first part is usually a request for God to grant the deceased a home in heaven[18]. This is often accompanied by an expression of certainty that it has already happened or is bound to happen. In the second part the speaker asks God to provide the person suffering after a loss with consolation. The parts of a supplement may be divided by a DM expression.

6.4.1. Supplement I > Blessing for the deceased

This occurs 369 times, i.e., in 43% of the comments. Multi-formulaic expressions are a characteristic of this slot. As the slot practically never occurs alone, the subject (God) expressed in the core is not repeated, and the sentence is introduced with the *wa/wi* conjunction. The most typical example is *wi yiskinu fasīḥ gannitu* 'and [may God] make him live in his vastest paradise'. Here, the S-K-N root, related to the concept of "inhabiting", appears as a causative verb – *yuskin (yiskin)* 'give home'. The optative function is played by an imperfective verb (the perfective forms only occur 3 times). Examples with the imperative are also relatively common. A pronoun-based object is most common in the third person, while the deceased person is directly addressed in only 7 examples. Paradise is referred to with the expression *fasīḥ gannitu* 'the vastest paradise' or *il-fardūs il-a'la min il-ganna* 'the greatest paradise', each of which may sometimes be slightly modified. The expression *asma manāzil il-ganna* 'the highest (most sublime) places in heaven', which appears only once, is a non-standard example in this context. In several examples, these conventional formulae are extended with additional formulaic expressions: *min ġēr ḥisāb wa lā sābiqa 'aḏāb* 'without being taken to account or torment', *ma' an-nabiyyīn wa ṣ-ṣadīqīn wa š-šuhadā' wa ṣ-ṣāliḥīn wa ḥusn ulāika rafīqan* 'the prophets, the

[18] "Heaven", "paradise", and "garden" are used interchangeably in the translation of Arabic names.

steadfast affirmers of truth, the martyrs and the righteous, and excellent are those as companions'[19] and *bi raḥmitak* 'with your mercy'.

Table 12. Supplement I, example 1

aḷḷāhum-ma 'Oh, God' (1)	*yiskin* 'give home' (139)	3rd (159)	*fasīḥ gannitu* 'the vastest paradise' (129)	*min ġēr ḥisāb wa lā sābiqa ʿaḏāb* 'without being taken to account or torment' (1)
rabbina 'Our Lord'(1)	*askin* 'give home' (24)	2nd (7)	*fasīḥ al-ginān* 'the vastest paradise' (1)	*maʿ an-nabiyyīn wa ṣ-ṣadīqīn wa š-šuhadāʾ wa ṣ-ṣāliḥīn wa ḥusn ulāika rafīqan* 'the prophets, the steadfast affirmers of truth, the martyrs and the righteous, and excellent are those as companions' (1)
	askan (3)		*fasīḥ gannitak* 'your vastest paradise' (9)	*bi raḥmitak* 'with your mercy' (1)
			il-fardūs il-a'la min il-ganna 'the greatest garden of heaven' (8)	
			il-fardūs il-a'la 'the greatest paradise' (12)	
			gannit il-fardūs il-ʾala 'the greatest garden of heaven' (1)	
			Il-fardūs 'paradise' (1)	
			il-ganna 'heaven' (3)	
			fasīḥ gannitu il-firdūs il-a'la min il-ganna 'his vastest paradise, the greatest garden of heaven' (1)	
			asma manāzil il-ganna 'the highest (most sublime) places in heaven' (1)	

[19] QS 4: 69. Sahih International translation.

The two examples below illustrate including one's relatives and all the Muslims as addressees of the blessing, which is relatively common and occurs occasionally in all the slots:

(117) *askanu fasīḥ gannitu wi waldi wi gamīʿ mawta l-muslimīn* 'May [God] make him live in his vastest paradise, him and my father and all deceased Muslims'.

(118) *askanu fasīḥ gannitu wi amwāt il-muslimīn agmaʿīn* 'May [God] make him live in his vastest paradise, and all deceased Muslims'.

Another large group of expressions uses predicates based on the verb *yigʿal* 'make'. Several conventional formulae to be distinguished here are shown in tables 13–17.

Table 13. Supplement I, example 2

<table>
<tr><td>yigʿal 'Make' (43)</td><td>maṯwa 'abode' +3rd (40)</td><td>il-ganna 'heaven' (41)</td><td>wi naʿimha 'and its bliss' (1)</td><td>bidūn ḥisāb wa lā sābiqa ʿaḏāb 'without being taken to account or torment' (1)</td></tr>
<tr><td rowspan="2">igʿal 'Make' (1)</td><td>maṯwa 'abode' + 2nd (2)</td><td colspan="3" rowspan="2">il-fardūs il-aʿla 'the greatest paradise' (3)</td></tr>
<tr><td>maʾwā 'refuge' + 3rd (2)</td></tr>
</table>

Table 13 encompasses 44 examples, the most typical of which is *yigʿal maṯwāh (maswāh) il-ganna* '(may he) make his abode heaven'. There is one example of an imperative verb. The first object is usually expressed with a noun phrase (NP) with a possessive pronoun relating to the deceased (in a vast majority, in the third person), this most commonly being *maṯwā/maswa* 'abode', *maʾwā* 'refuge' occurring only twice. The second object is a reference to the paradise (most commonly *al-ǧanna/il-ganna*). Additionally, one example not included in the table occurs with an unusual word order:

(119) *yigʿal il-ganna maʾwāhum* 'May [God] make heaven their refuge'.

Similarly to the core, he author of the comment may also happen to add their relatives to the supplication. In the following example the word *abī* 'my father' suggest the standard variant (unlike the dialectal *abūya*).

(120) *yigʿal maswāh il-ganna (yaǧʿal maṯwāhu l-ǧanna) huwa wa abī wa kull ʿazīzī* 'May [God] make his abode heaven, him and my father, and every dear person'.

Table 14. Supplement I, example 3

rabbina 'Our Lord' (1)	*yig'al* 'make' (10)	*'abr* 'grave' + 3rd (15)	*rawḍa min riyāḍ il-ganna* 'a garden from the gardens of paradise' (15)
aḷḷāhumma 'Oh, God' (2)	*ig'al* 'make' (5)		

Another example is the expression *yig'al/ig'al 'abru rawḍa min riyāḍ il-ganna* 'May [God] make his grave a garden from the gardens of paradise', which occurs 15 times. This time, there was not even one verb in the perfective form among the examples analysed. Additionally, there were 3 cases of explicitly expressed subject (agent) – once as *rabbina* 'our Lord' and twice in the vocative *aḷḷāhumma* form. One of the examples quotes a phrase from a Hadith[20]:

(121) *rabbina yağ'al qabarahu rawḍa min riyāḍ al-ğānna wa lā ḥufra min ḥufr an-nār* 'Oh, God, make his grave a garden from the gardens of paradise, not a pit from the pits of the fire'.

As can be observed in the example below, the vocative expression *aḷḷāhumma* may appear as an interjection after the predicate, which is not a typical decision. Moreover, the aforementioned extension of the supplication to one's relatives and all the Muslims can be observed here.

(122) *ig'al aḷḷāhumma 'abraha rawḍa min riyāḍ il-ganna (iğ'āl aḷḷāhumma qabaraha rawḍa min riyāḍ al-ğanna) wa ummī wa abī wa iẖwatī wa amwāt al-muslimīn* 'Make, oh God, her grave a garden from the gardens of paradise, as well as my mother, father, my siblings, and all deceased Muslims'.

This expression exhibits high connectivity with the phrase *yinawwar 'abru* 'illuminate his grave', which appears 8 times in the material studied, e.g.:

(123) *wi yinawwar 'abraha wi yag'alu rawḍa min riyāḍ il-ganna* 'Illuminate her grave and make it a garden from the gardens of paradise'.

Table 15. Supplement I, example 4

rabbina 'Our Lord' (2)	*yinawwar* 'illuminate' (10)	*'abr* 'grave' + 3rd (10)

Another group of expressions, with the G-'-L root, locates the deceased among the inhabitants of heaven. In this case, imperfective examples yet again prove

[20] Jami' at-Tirmiḏī, Book 37, Hadith 2460, retrieved from: https://sunnah.com/tirmidhi, access: April 2021.

most common, with a single occurrence of the imperative. The word *rabbina* ‘our Lord’ occurs twice, while other sentences are devoid of a subject. A prototypical sentence in this group is *wi yigʿalu min ahl il-ganna* ‘may [God] make him one of the dwellers of paradise’.

Table 16. Supplement I, example 5

<table>
<tr><td rowspan="2">rabbina ‘Our Lord’ (2)</td><td>yigʿal ‘make’ (18)</td><td>3rd (18)</td><td rowspan="2">min ahl ‘one of the people’ (19)</td><td>il-ganna ‘heaven’ (14)</td><td>wi naʿimha ‘and its bliss’ (1)</td></tr>
<tr><td>igʿal ‘make’ (1)</td><td>2nd (1)</td><td>il-fardūs il-aʿla ‘the greatest garden’ (5)</td><td>min il-ganna ‘of heaven’ (1)</td></tr>
</table>

A similar example is illustrated in table 17, but here the PP with *min (ahl)* ‘one of [the people]’ is replaced by a PP with the preposition *fi* ‘in’. Such formulae also locate the deceased among the inhabitants of heaven, such as e.g. martyrs, or in “the high level of heaven”: *aʿlā d-daraǧāt* ‘the highest level’, *al-firdaws al-aʿlā (il-fardūs il-aʿla)* ‘the greatest garden’.

Table 17. Supplement I, example 6

<table>
<tr><td rowspan="5">rabbina ‘Our Lord’ (2)</td><td rowspan="5">yigʿal ‘make’ (6)</td><td rowspan="5">3rd (6)</td><td>fi manzil aš-šuhadāʾ wa ṣ-ṣadīqīn ‘in the house of martyrs and friends’ (1)</td><td rowspan="5">min ġayr ḥisāb wa lā ʿaḏāb ‘without being taken to account or torment’ (1)</td></tr>
<tr><td>fi mīzān ḥasanātihi ‘in the scale of his good deeds’ (2)</td></tr>
<tr><td>al-firdaws al-aʿlā min ‘the greatest garden of’ (1)</td></tr>
<tr><td>al-firdaws al-aʿlā maʿa ṣ-ṣadīqīn wa š-šuhadāʾ wa ḥusn ulāʾika rafīqan ‘in the greatest paradise with the steadfast affirmers of truth, the martyrs, and excellent are those as companions’ (1)</td></tr>
<tr><td>aʿlā d-daraǧāt ‘the highest level’ (2)</td></tr>
</table>

(124) *rabbina yigʿalu fi aʿla d-daragāt* 'May our Lord make him [be] in the highest level'.

The above table shows the more ornate examples among the supplements. One of them was additionally enriched with the expression *min ġayr ḥisāb wa lā ʿaḏāb* 'without being taken to account or torment', which occurs multiple times in the material studied.

Table 18 shows another set of formulae, this time based on the D-Ḫ-L root. It constitutes the basis of the causative verb *adḫal/yudḫil* 'let in'. Similarly to the previous groups, the most common verbal forms are imperfective ones with a third-person singular pronoun as an object. In only five instances the predicate is perfective. Yet again, the expressions *fasīḥ gannitu* 'the vastest paradise' and *il-fardūs il-aʿla* 'the greatest garden' are most commonly used to refer to paradise. As was the case above, a request for the deceased to be admitted to paradise without judgement and without suffering occurs twice.

Table 18. Supplement I, example 7

<table>
<tr><td rowspan="7">rabbina 'Our Lord' (1)</td><td>yudḫil 'let in' (15)</td><td>3rd (20)</td><td>fasīḥ gannitu 'the vastest paradise' (10)</td><td>bidūn ḥisāb wa lā sābiqa ʿaḏāb 'without being taken to account or torment' (1)</td></tr>
<tr><td>adḫal 'let in' (5)</td><td rowspan="6">2nd (1)</td><td>fasīḥ gannitak 'your vastest paradise' (1)</td><td rowspan="6">bidūn ḥisāb 'without being taken to account' (1)</td></tr>
<tr><td rowspan="5">adḫil 'let in' (1)</td><td>il-ganna 'heaven' (3)</td></tr>
<tr><td>il-fardūs il-aʿla 'the greatest garden' (5)</td></tr>
<tr><td>il-fardūs il-aʿla min il-ganna 'the greatest garden of heaven' (1)</td></tr>
<tr><td>gannit il-fardūs il-aʿla 'the greatest garden of heaven' (1)</td></tr>
<tr></tr>
</table>

Another group of expressions represents an identical construction with the root R-Z-ʾ 'bestow', where a typical example is the sentence: *yurzuʾu l-ganna* 'may [God] bestow upon him (a place in) paradise' / *yurzuʾu l-fardūs il-aʿla* 'may [God] bestow upon him [a place in] the greatest paradise'.

Table 19. Supplement I, example 8

aḷḷāhumma 'Oh, God' (3)	*yurzuʾ* 'bestow upon' (14)	3rd (18)	*il-ganna* 'heaven' (7)	*wa n-naʿīm* 'and bliss' (1)	*bi ġēr ḥisāb* 'without being taken to account' (2)	*wa lā sābiqa ʿaḏāb* 'or torment' (1)
	urzuʾ 'be-stow upon' (4)		*il-fardūs il-aʿla* 'the greatest paradise (9)	*min al-ganna (1)*	*bi izni ḷḷāh* 'with God's permission' (3)	
			naʿimha 'its bliss' (1)			
			fūʾ in-naʿīm naʿīm 'bliss beyond all blisses' (1)			

In example (125) below, a description of paradise is replaced by the emphatic expression: *fūʾ in-naʿīm naʿīm* 'bliss beyond all blisses'. The next example is not typical for the group. Paradise here is referred to as the "vicinity/closeness" of the prophet Muhammad, here called *muṣṭafā* 'the chosen one'.

(125) *aḷḷāhumma rzuʾu fūʾ in-naʿīm naʿīm* 'Oh, God, bestow upon him bliss that is beyond all blisses'.

(126) *yarzuquhā ǧiwār al-muṣṭafā ṣallā ʿalayhi wa sallam* 'May [God] grant her the neighbourhood of the chosen one, peace be upon him'.

A separate group involves examples of the following type: *fi l-ganna in šāʾ aḷḷāh* 'in heaven, God willing', *fi l-ganna wa naʿimha bi izni llāh* 'in heaven and its bliss with God's permission', which (with the exception of four) are not sentences. Three examples from this group include the verbs *yikūn* 'be', *yinʿam* 'bask in'. One example is a nominal sentence with a personal pronoun as the subject. The pragmatic function of those expressions is optative, even though formally they are mostly statements expressing certainty. The expressions *in šāʾ aḷḷāh* 'God willing' (most often) and *bi izni llāh* 'with God's permission' are a characteristic element adhering to this group, which is illustrated in example (127).

Table 20. Supplement I, example 9

yikūn 'Be' *(2)*	*fi l-ganna wi naʿimha* 'in heaven and its bliss' (7)	*in šā' aḷḷāh* 'God willing' (13)
	fi l-ganna 'in heaven' (5)	*bi izni llāh* 'with God's permission' (2)
huwwa 'He' (1)	*fi gannit al-ḫald* 'in the eternal paradise' (1)	
yanʿam 'Bask in' (1)	*fi ğannat aḷḷāh* 'in the garden of God' (1)	
	fi gannāt in-naʿīm 'in the garden of bliss' (3)	
	fi a'la makān fi l-fardūs il-a'la 'in the highest place of the greatest garden' (1)	
	maʿa š-šuhadā' 'with martyrs' (1)	

(127) *in šā' aḷḷāh fi l-ganna wa naʿimha* 'God willing, in heaven and its bliss'.
(128) *yanʿam al-ān fi ğannat aḷḷāh* 'He is now basking in God's heaven'.

The expressions take the form of statements but are obviously pragmatically oriented as blessings. We will find similar expressions in the examples (129) and (130), which, due to their non-formulaic (or partially non-formulaic) nature, were not included in the table above.

(129) *sirtik il-ḥilwa wi ʿamalik iṭ-ṭayyib hayiftaḥlik abwāb il-ganna* 'Your beautiful story and your good deeds will open for you the door of heaven'.
(130) *hiya l-ān fi ğiwār al-ḥannān al-mannān* 'She is now in the neighbourhood of the Merciful, the Benefactor'.

The following table shows the concept of joining the deceased in the life to come. The construction is based on the verb *yigmaʿ* 'unite', which occurs in the imperfective form in all the examples studied. Interestingly, in some comments from this group, the beneficiary of the blessing is not only the addressee of the comment, but sometimes the authors also counts themselves in.

(131) *rabbina yigmaʿna bihum fi l-ganna in šā' aḷḷāh* 'May our Lord unite us with them in heaven, God willing'.

Table 21. Supplement I, example 10

<table>
<tr><td rowspan="9">rabbina ‘Our Lord’ (4)</td><td rowspan="9">yigma‘ ‘unite’ (16)</td><td>1st PL (8)</td><td>bi + 3rd (12)</td><td>fi l-ganna ‘in heaven’ (6)</td><td>in šā’ aḷḷāh ‘God willing’ (3)</td><td rowspan="9">‘ala ḫēr ‘well’ (3)</td></tr>
<tr><td>2nd SG (2)</td><td rowspan="8">bi + kinship term (4)</td><td>fi gannāt an-na‘īm ‘in the garden of bliss’ (3)</td><td rowspan="8">bi izni llāh ‘with God’s permission’ (2)</td></tr>
<tr><td>2nd PL (2)</td><td>fi ğannatihi mustaqirr raḥmatihi ‘in his garden, the abiding abode of his mercy’ (1)</td></tr>
<tr><td rowspan="6">3rd (4)</td><td>fi mustaqirr raḥmatihi ‘in the abiding abode of his mercy’ (1)</td></tr>
<tr><td>‘andu fi d-daragāt il-a‘la min il-ganna bi giwār sayyidna muḥammad il-muḫtār ṣallā aḷḷāh ‘alēh ‘in his home in the highest level of heaven in the neighbourhood of Muhammad, the chosen one, peace be upon him’ (1)</td></tr>
<tr><td>fi gannāt wa nahr wa maq‘ad ṣidq mālik muqtadir ‘in the midst of gardens and rivers in an assembly of truth, in the presence of a sovereign omnipotent’[21] (1)</td></tr>
<tr><td>fi l- āḫira ‘in the afterlife’ (1)</td></tr>
<tr><td>fi l-fardūs il-a‘la min il-ganna ‘in the highest garden of heaven’ (1)</td></tr>
<tr><td>fi gannit il-ma’wa ‘in the garden of refuge’ (1)</td></tr>
</table>

The examples (132–134) illustrate the expressions appearing in this group:

(132) *yigma‘hum fi gannit il-ma’wa in šā’ aḷḷāh* ‘May [God] unite them in the garden of refuge, God willing’.

(133) *yigma‘ha bi awladha fi l-fardūs il-a‘la min il-ganna* ‘May [God] unite her with her children in the greatest garden of heaven’.

(134) *rabbina yigma‘na bīhum fi gannāt in-na‘īm* ‘May Lord unite us with them in the garden of bliss’.

In the example below, *in šā’ aḷḷāh* ‘God willing’ is used exceptionally as an interjection:

(135) *yigma‘na bīhum in šā’ aḷḷāh fi l-ganna* ‘May [God] unite us with them, God willing, in heaven’.

[21] Q54:55.

The same idea is also sometimes expressed with the verb *yulḥi'* 'cause to join', which occurs 6 times in the material studied:

(136) *yulḥi'na bīh 'ala ḫēr* 'May [God] make us join him [well]'.

(137) *yulḥi'na bīh wi bi aḥbabna 'āla ḫēr* 'May [God] make us join him and our loved ones [well]'.

(138) *alḥi'na bīh fi ṣ-ṣaliḥīn* 'May [God] make us join him in heaven [with the righteous]'.

(139) *alḥi'na bi ṣ-ṣaliḥīn* 'May [God] make us join the righteous'.

One example is distinct among others. It features the verb *yig'al* 'make':

(140) *rabbina yig'allina liqā' bīkum fi l-fardūs il-a'la* 'May our Lord make us meet you in the greatest paradise'.

The following roots also appear among rare forms: R-F-' (7 times), H-S-N (4 times), Ṯ-B-T (4 times), K-R-M (twice), N-Z-L (twice), Ḥ-Š-R (once), Q-B-L (once). The verbs with the R-F-' root constitute a group of forms referring to the deceased person's place in heaven – the author uses them to ask God to place the deceased in a high level of heaven.

(141) *yirfa' daragtu fi l-ganna* 'May [God] elevate his position in heaven'.

(142) *yirfa'ak li a'la daragāt il-ganna* 'May God elevate you onto the highest level of heaven'.

(143) *yirfa' manziltik min il-ganna* 'May [God] elevate your position in heaven'.

The verb *yuḥsin* 'bestow good' which previously occurred in core II, here expresses a request for the future dwelling or shelter of the deceased to be of the best kind possible:

(144) *yuḥsin mudḫalu* 'Make his entry a good one'.

(145) *yuḥsin maswāh* 'Make his abode a good one'.

(146) *yuḥsin nuzluhum* 'Make their resting place a good one'.

(147) *yuḥsin ḫātimitna* 'Make our end a good one'.

The root K-R-M refers to divine generosity:

(148) *akrimu bi l-ganna wa na'imha* 'Grant him [a place in] heaven and its bliss'.

(149) *akrim nuzlaha* 'Make her resting place a noble one'.

The verb *yunzil* 'give home' creates sentences synonymous with those using the verb *yiskin*, referring to the concept of "giving dwelling". Only one sentence with the verb *yataqabbal* 'accept' occurred in this slot, similarly to the verb *yaḥšur* 'crowd together':

(150) *anzilhu l-fardūs il-a'la min il-ganna* 'Give him home in the greatest garden of heaven'.

(151) *anzilhum manzilit aṣ-ṣadīqīn wa n-nabiyyīn* 'Give them place in the house of friends and martyrs'.
(152) *taqabbalha fī fasīḥ gannitu* 'May [God] accept her in his vastest paradise'.
(153) *yaḥšurak ma'a ṣ-ṣadīqīn wa š-šuhadā'* 'May [God] join you with friends and martyrs'.

A formula of slightly different meaning occurs four times:
(154) *yisabbitu 'ind is-su'āl* 'May [God] keep him strong when he is asked [by the angels]'[22].

This expression is a request for strengthening the deceased on Judgement Day, when, according to the Muslim faith, two angels will descend upon his grave and question them about their faith.

6.4.2. Supplement II > Blessing for the mourner

This slot occurs 207 times in the corpus, i.e., in 24,1% of the comments. Here, the author of the comment is asking God for consolation for somebody who is suffering after the loss of a person close to them. The dominant concept is *ṣabr* 'patience', expressed with verbs *yiṣabbar* 'soothe', 'give patience', *yilhim* 'inspire' or *yurzuq* 'bestow'. Examples which follow the concept of God giving *ṣabr* on a sufferer constitute as many as 92%.

Table 22. Supplement II, example 1

rabbina 'Our Lord' (27)	*yiṣabbar* 'give patience' (170)	2nd (87)	*'ala furā'* 'after the loss' + 3rd (23)	*ṣabran ǧamīlan* 'beautiful patience' (1)
aḷḷāh 'God' (1)		*ahl* 'family' + 2nd (3)	*'ala l-furā'* 'after the loss' (2)	
		'alb 'heart' + 2nd (24)	*'ala l-ayyam al-qalīla bidūnikum* 'during these few days without them' (1)	
		ahl 'family' + 3rd (39)	*'ala maṣābik* 'after the tragedy' (1)	
		kinship term/term of endearment + 3rd (10)		
		1st (7)		

22 Referring to the Islamic belief that a dead person, while still in grave, will have to answer three questions asked by the angels: Nakīr and Munkar, about his/her God, prophet and faith.

Predicates with the verb *yiṣabbar* 'give patience' occur in imperfective forms only. The subject is explicitly expressed only in 28 examples, while most often it is *rabbina*, which suggests that on the dialect-standard scale, such expressions are closer to the dialectal pole. The most typical sentence in this compilation is (155) or (156). It is also relatively often that examples with objects such as in (157) can be found:

(155) *wi yiṣabbarak* 'And [may he] give you patience'.
(156) *wi yiṣabbar ahlu* 'And [may he] give his family patience'.
(157) *rabbina yiṣabbar ʾalbik* 'May Lord soothe your heart'.

Among the examples analysed, 27 are extended with a further phrase, *ʿala l-furāʾ* 'after/because of the loss' or a similar one. In addition to that, one example includes a *muṭlaq* type of structure: *ṣabran ğamīlan* 'beautiful patience'.

Sentences with the verb *yulhim* 'inspire' are definitely rarer. They take objects in the second person (usually pronouns) and the third person (generally NPs). Those are conventional formulae of the following type:

(158) *wi yulhim ahluhum wi zawīhum iṣ-ṣabr wi s-silwān* 'And may [God] inspire her family and relatives with patience and consolation'.
(159) *wi yulhimik iṣ-ṣabr* 'And may [God] inspire you with patience'.

Table 23. Supplement II, example 2

rabbina 'Our Lord' (1)	*yulhim* 'inspire' (19)	*ahl* 'family' +3rd(10)	*wi zawī* 'and relatives' + 3rd (3)	*iṣ-ṣabr* 'patience' (19)	*wi s-silwān* 'and consolation' (9)
		2nd (9)	*gamīʿan* 'all' (1)		

The last group to be distinguished among the formulae with the central concept of *ṣabr* are expressions with the verb *yurzuʾ* 'grant'. But a few examples are present here, each with an object in the form of a second-person pronoun.

Table 24. Supplement II, example 3

yurzuʾ 'Grant' (2)	2nd (3)	*iṣ-ṣabr* 'patience' (3)	*ʾala l-furāʾ* 'after the loss' (1)
urzuʾ 'Grant' (1)			

(160) *yurzuʾik iṣ-ṣabr ʾala l-furāʾ* 'May [God] give you patience after the loss'.

Another uniform group of expressions are requests for God to strengthen "the heart" of a person mourning after the loss of a loved one. The verb *yarbiṭ* 'give strength'[23] with an object in the form of PP occurs here.

Table 25. Supplement II, example 4

yarbiṭ 'Give strength' (7)	*'ala 'alb / 'ala 'ulūb* 'to heart' (8)	+ 2nd (4)
irbiṭ 'Give strength' (1)		+3rd (4)

(161) *yarbiṭ 'ala 'albik* 'May [God] give strength to your heart'.
(162) *yarbiṭ 'ala 'ulubkum* 'May [God] give strength to your hearts'.

Table 26. Supplement II, example 5

aḷḷāh 'God' (1)	*yi'awwi* 'strengthen' (4)	2nd (3)	*'ala furā'* 'after the loss' + 3rd (1)
rabbina 'Our Lord' (1)		3rd (1)	*'ala l-furā'* 'after the loss' (1)

The last group are requests for strength for the sufferer with the *yi'awwi* 'strengthen' verb, occurring in similar constructions as before.
(163) *yi'awwiha 'ala l-furā'* 'May [God] make you strong after the loss'.
(164) *rabbina yi'awwiki* 'May our Lord make you strong'.

The material also includes a single example with the verb *yiṯabbit (yisabbit)* 'reinforce':
(165) *wi yisabbitik* 'And may [God] reinforce you'.

The material studied includes several examples in which the speaker is asking God for patience for themselves as well, thus positioning themselves on the same level as the mourner.
(166) *ya rabb yiṣabbarna* 'Oh, Lord, [may he] give us patience'.

This slot also includes multi-formulaic expressions, in which rare or even unconventional forms can be found. One may fall under the impression that the multiplication

[23] This formula originates from a Quranic verse 18:14 starting with words: *wa rabaṭnā 'alā qulūbihim* 'We gave strength to their hearts'.

of successive blessings is supposed to generate a pragmatic effect of amplifying the message. The use of rare and sophisticated formulae, a classicising style and a skilful juxtaposition of formulae of religious origin all probably serve a similar function.

(167) *yiṣabbar ahlaha wi yiʿinhum wi yiʾawwīhum* 'May [God] give her family patience, console them and make them strong'.

(168) *yunzil bard as-sakīna wa r-riḍāʾ ʿala qulūb kull aḥibbāʾihi* 'May [God] send the cold of peace and acceptance on the hearts of all his loved ones'.

(169) *wa mā ṣabrak illa min ʿind aḷḷāh* 'And your patience is not but trough God'[24].

6.5. Framing formula > Death-related expression

A framing formula at the end of a comment occurs 12 times, so in a mere 1.4%. It encompasses the same formulae as at the beginning, yet, due to the low number of occurrences, they are less varied.

Table 27. Framing formula

al-baqāʾ li llāh 'Only God is eternal' (3)
al-baqāʾ wi d-dawām li llāh 'The eternity and perpetuity belong to God' (1)
inna li ḷḷāh wa inna ilayhi ragiʿūn 'Verily we belong to God and verily to him do we return' (8)

6.6. Closing formula > General reference to God

There are only 4 occurrences of expressions in this slot (0.5%) and they represent one formula *lā ḥawl wa lā quwwa illa bi ḷḷāh* 'there is no power and no strength save in God'. Additionally, this formula once occurs in an extended version and once in a shortened version.

Table 28. Closing formula

lā ḥawl wa lā quwwa illa bi ḷḷāh 'There is no power and no strength save in God' (3)	*il-ʿali l-ʿaẓīm* 'the highest, the greatest' (1)
lā quwwa illa bi ḷḷāh 'There is no strength save in God' (1)	

[24] This is a distorted version of Quranic: *wa ṣbir wa mā ṣabruka illā bi ḷḷāhi* 'and be patient and your patience is not but trough God' Q16:127.

Taking into account the small number of closing formulae and framing formulae occurring after the key part of the utterance, one ought to deem them a relatively rare alternative for the same expressions occurring at the beginning.

6.7. A special case

In most of the comments studied, the experience of death is described as natural for a human being. The comments are dominated by religious optics and focused on eternal life. It is rare that the tragedy of death is emphasised, and only exceptionally can one find the speakers expressing their sadness – such comments occur particularly in the non-formulaic material presented at the end of this chapter. Against such a background, there is a special case indeed to be observed in comments below, a group of posts announcing the death of a young woman, preceded by a year-long separation from her children, who had been kidnapped by their father. The woman developed severe depression and died from emotionally induced health complications. The condolences for her mother and friends often assume a characteristic form. In addition to the core, the supplement, and other forms distinguished before, there appear a formulaic reference to the tragedy which the woman experienced and curses addressed to both her former husband and her mother-in-law, who also played a part in her suffering, accompanied by requests for God to make up for the misfortunes she had to endure in life.

6.7.1. Reaction to news about the tragedy

The basic formula used in this context is the Quranic verse (3:173) *ḥasbī ḷḷāh wa niʿma l-wakīl* 'God is sufficient for me and he is the best disposer of affairs' or *ḥasbunā ḷḷāh wa niʿma l-wakīl* 'God is sufficient for us and he is the best disposer of affairs'[25] occurring in the framing formula spot (before or after the core), sometimes together with the framing formula. This expression is commonly in the Islamic world "recommended" in moments of fear and helplessness and when facing a tragedy.

These 29 comments offer further specification, usually discussing the woman's husband, often referred to as *ẓalim*, and the cause of her suffering.

(170) *ḥasbi ḷḷāh wa niʿma l-wakīl fi guzha wi mamtu* 'God is sufficient for me and he is the best disposer of affairs against her husband and his mom'.

(171) *ḥasbina ḷḷāh wa niʿma l-wakīl fi man ẓalamha wa ḥaramha min al-awlād* 'God is sufficient for us and he is the best disposer of affairs against those who oppressed her and deprived her of her children'.

[25] Both formulae are transcribed in their dialectalised variants in most examples.

Table 29. Reaction to the tragedy

<table>
<tr><td>ḥasbi ḷḷāh wa ni'ma l-wakīl 'God is sufficient for me and he is the best disposer of affairs' (64)</td><td rowspan="11">fi (29)</td><td rowspan="5">kull (13)</td><td>ẓālim 'oppressor' (6)</td></tr>
<tr><td rowspan="10">ḥasbina ḷḷāh wa ni'ma l-wakīl 'God is sufficient for us and he is the best disposer of affairs' (18)</td><td>man tasabbab fī qahriha 'who made her suffer' (1)</td></tr>
<tr><td>ab yiḥrim umm min awladha 'father depriving a mother of her children' (2)</td></tr>
<tr><td>illi ẓalamha 'who oppressed her' (3)</td></tr>
<tr><td>rāgil ẓālim 'oppressive man' (1)</td></tr>
<tr><td>guzha 'her husband' (3)</td><td>wi mamtu 'his mom' (1)</td></tr>
<tr><td colspan="2">ṭali'ha 'her former husband'(1)</td></tr>
<tr><td colspan="2">man ẓalamha wa ḥaramha min al-awlād 'who oppressed her and deprived her of the children' (1)</td></tr>
<tr><td colspan="2">illi ẓalam 'who oppressed [her]' (1)</td></tr>
<tr><td rowspan="2">3rd (10)</td><td>huwwa wi ummu 'him and his mother' (1)</td></tr>
<tr><td>wi filli zayyu 'and who resembles him' (1)</td></tr>
</table>

Generalisations with the pronoun *kull*, which connect the content of the comment to all people who act similarly, are of particular interest here. Situation (173), however, is exceptional, as the author elaborates on the behaviour of one specific person in spite of the generalisation being applied as well.

(172) *ḥasbi ḷḷāh wa ni'ma l-wakīl fi kull ẓalim* 'God is sufficient for me and he is the best disposer of affairs' against every oppressor'.

(173) *ḥasbina ḷḷāh wa ni'ma l-wakīl fi kull ab yiḥrim umm min awaldha* 'God is sufficient for us, and he is the best disposer of affairs against every father depriving a mother of her children'.

The two following situations present (174) a shortening of a formula – the only such case in the material studied. While most formulae used in condolences have, as already illustrated, rather loose structure and modifications that are acceptable to a varying extent, Quranic verses are treated with particular pietism.

(174) *ḥasbi ḷḷāh 'a l-kulli ẓālim* 'God is sufficient for me against every oppressor'.

In the latter case, we can see a few repetitions of a formula – this time without any modifications, which provides a stylistic effect of recitation. Such operations are, in turn, relatively common in the material studied.

(175) *ḥasbi ḷḷāh wa niʿma l-wakīl, ḥasbi ḷḷāh wa niʿma l-wakīl, ḥasbi ḷḷāh wa niʿma l-wakīl* 'God is sufficient for me, and he is the best disposer of affairs, God is sufficient for me, and he is the best disposer of affairs, God is sufficient for me, and he is the best disposer of affairs'.

6.7.2. Blessing for the deceased

Another characteristic type of reaction are blessings, of which the most often repeated is the hope that in heaven God compensates the deceased for the suffering she went through in her life. The only structurally coherent group of blessings is noted around the verb *yiʿawwiḍ* 'compensate'.

Table 30. Blessing with the verb *yiʿawwiḍ*

<table>
<tr><td rowspan="4">rabbina 'Our Lord' (4)</td><td rowspan="4">yiʿawwiḍ 'compensate' (11)</td><td>3rd (8)</td><td colspan="2">ʿan kull alam šafitu fi d-dinya 'for all the pain she experienced [saw] in her life' (1)</td><td rowspan="4">fi l-ganna w naʿimha 'in heaven and its bliss' (1)</td></tr>
<tr><td rowspan="3">2nd (3)</td><td colspan="2">ʿan kull it-taʿab wi l-qahr 'for all the pain and suffering' (1)</td></tr>
<tr><td colspan="2">ḫēr 'well' (4)</td></tr>
<tr><td>bi l-ganna 'in heaven' (4)</td><td>bi izni ḷḷāh 'with God's permission' (1)</td></tr>
</table>

(176) *rabbina yiʿawwiḍha ḫēr* 'May Lord compensate it for her well'.

(177) *rabbina yiʿawwiḍha wi yiḥfiẓ awladha* 'May Lord compensate it for her and keep her children safe'.

(178) *yiʿawwiḍik ḫēr wi yurzuʾik zōg afḍal min zawgik wa ahlān afḍal min ahlik* 'May [God] compensate it for you well and give you a husband better that your husband and family better than your family'.

In (178), we can see a fragment of a prayer beginning with a dialectal blessing. Such diglossic switching is characteristic for the whole material, just like quoting prayers (*duʿāʾ*). The prayer: *abdilhā dāran ḫayran min dārihā wa ahlan ḫayran min ahlihā* 'give her in exchange a home better than her home (on earth) and a family better than her family' is adjusted to the current situation – *yurzuʾik zōg afḍal* 'may [God] give you a better husband'. Other blessings include:

(179) *rabbina yirḍīha ʿandu* 'May Lord make her happy in his home'.
(180) *aḷḷāhumma abdilhā dāran ḫayran min dārihā wa ahlan ḫayran min ahlihā* 'Oh, God, give her in exchange a home better than her home [on earth] and a family better than her family'.
(181) *wa kull mā ʿānathu fī mīzān ḥasanātihā* 'And everything she suffered will be added to the account of her good deeds'.

6.7.3. Curse

It is common that part of the comment consists of a curse directed against the former husband of the deceased girl and (sometimes) his mother or ones who behaved like him. In the most common scenario, the author of the comment asks God to take revenge on him: *rabbina yintiʾim minnu* 'may our Lord take revenge on him'.

Table 31. Curse with the verb *yintiʾim* 'take revenge'

<table>
<tr><td>rabbina 'Our Lord' (28)</td><td rowspan="12">yintiʾim min 'take revenge on' (43)</td><td rowspan="3">3rd (26)</td><td>huwwa wa ummu 'him and his mother' (1)</td><td>ašadd intiqām 'the most severe revenge' (1)</td></tr>
<tr><td rowspan="11">ya rabb 'Oh, Lord' (1)</td><td>wi min ayy ḥadd saʿdu ʿala ẓ-ẓulm da 'and on everyone who helped him in this oppression' (1)</td><td rowspan="11">aglan aw ʿāgilan 'sooner or later' (2)</td></tr>
<tr><td>wi min amsālu 'and on people like him' (1)</td></tr>
<tr><td colspan="2">kull ẓālim 'every oppressor' (6)</td></tr>
<tr><td colspan="2">kull man ẓalam + 3rd 'everyone who oppressed' (2)</td></tr>
<tr><td colspan="2">kull man kān lu īd fi ḥuznaha wi alamha 'everyone who contributed to her sadness and pain' (1)</td></tr>
<tr><td colspan="2">kull man yiḥrim wa yamnaʿ ḥuʾūʾ in-nās 'on everyone who violates other people's rights' (1)</td></tr>
<tr><td colspan="2">man ẓalam 'who oppressed' + 2nd (2)</td></tr>
<tr><td colspan="2">ṭalīʾha 'her former husband' (1)</td></tr>
<tr><td colspan="2">iẓ-ẓalama 'the oppressors' (1)</td></tr>
<tr><td colspan="2">illi ḥaramha min wiladha wi lli saʿdu 'who deprived her of her children and helped him' (2)</td></tr>
<tr><td colspan="2">man ḥaramahā an taḥtaḍin awlādahā 'who deprived her of holding her children' (1)</td></tr>
</table>

(182) *hayinti'im minnu aglan aw ʿāgilan* '[God] will take revenge on him sooner or later'.
(183) *rabbina yinti'im min kull min kān lu īd fi ḥuznaha wi alamha* 'May our Lord take revenge on everyone who contributed to her sadness and pain'.
(184) *rabbina yinti'im minnu wi yišūf illi hiyya šafitu* 'May our Lord take revenge on him and let him see what she saw'.
(185) *rabbina yantaqim mimman ḥaramahā an taḥtaḍin awlādahā* 'May our Lord take revenge on those who deprived her of holding her children'.

There is only one example with a verb in the imperative form in the text:
(186) *aḷḷāhumma nti'im min kulli ẓālim ṭāġi* 'Oh, God, take revenge on every oppressive tyrant'.

Among other examples of cursing, one might mention:
(187) *yiwaggaʿ 'ulubhum zayy ma waggaʿu 'albik wi azūki* 'May [God] make their hearts suffer just like they did to your heart and hurt you'.
(188) *yaḫudhum aḫz ʿazīz muqtadir* 'May [God] seize them with such penalty [as comes] from one exalted in power able to carry out his will'[26].
(189) *aḷḷāh yitṣarraf fīh* 'May God treat him [properly]'.

Another way is to assure that divine revenge is inevitable and to praise God's justice as that of the mightiest avenger, which has the same pragmatic power as a curse:
(190) *rabbina huwwa l-munta'im il-gabbār* 'Our Lord is a mighty avenger'.
(191) *inna ḷḷāhu l-muntaqim al-ʿādil* 'God is a just avenger'.
(192) *yumhil wa lā yuhmil, huwa l-muntagim al-ǧabbār* 'God's mill grinds slow but sure, our Lord is a mighty avenger'.

Table 32. God as avenger

rabbina 'Our Lord' (5)	*huwa/huwwa* 'he' (3)	*al-muntaqim/il-munta'im* 'avenger' (8)	*al-ʿādil* 'just' (1)
inna ḷḷāh 'Verily, God' (1)			*al-ǧabbār/il-gabbār* 'mighty' (6)

Statements of neutral value are similarly supposed to proclaim divine justice:
(193) *yiʿṭi kull wāḥid ʿala 'add ʿamalu* '[God] will reward every man according to his deeds'.

---

26 Q54:42, translation: Yusuf Ali.

Curses other than those based on the concept of revenge include swear words (including conventional and non-conventional ones, as well as other expressions, formulaic to varying extents):

(194) *bašširu guzha innu ḍamman ma"adu fi d-dark il-asfal ma' abu gahl* 'Inform her husband that he guaranteed his place in the lowest part [of the fire] with Abu Gahl'[27].

(195) *li yiḥya huwwa fi n-nār* 'May he live in hell'.

(196) *inti fakra inn rabbina hayatruk qāṭi' ar-raḥm ḥašan li llāh?* 'Do you think that our Lord will leave the one who cuts the ties of blood [unpunished]? God forbid!'

(197) *rabbina yigazīh huwwa wi ummu* 'May Lord repay him and his mother'.

(198) *rabbina yiḥrimu min ir-rāḥa wi min ir-raḥma wi yidū' ṭa'm il-garīma lli 'amalha la ḥadd ma yudḫul il-'abr* 'May Lord deprive him of comfort and mercy, may he be tasting the crime he committed until he enters the tomb'.

(199) *ya waylu min rabbina huwwa willi sa'du 'ala kida* 'Woe unto him and those who helped him'.

(200) *la'nit aḷḷāh 'alēh wi 'ala 'arību* 'God's curse on him and his relative'.

The construction of these expressions sometimes reflects curses, where the author of the utterance appeals to divine agency and calls for punishment for the one who had made the woman suffer; sometimes classical borrowings occur as well: *ya waylu* 'woe' and *la'nit aḷḷāh* 'God's curse'. There are also relatively common dialogic examples, where the author addresses the community of other posters or refers to other comments. Yet another form of reacting is the colloquial expression *minnu lillah* 'may he go to hell [may God punish him]' which occurs in the material four times.

6.8. Further features of the material

The examples below show comments containing formulae of a typical structure using the most common expressions (opening/framing formulae + core + supplement):

(201) *lā ḥawl wa lā quwwa illa bi ḷḷāh, rabbina yirḥamu wi yiġfirlu wi yig'al maswāh il-ganna wi yiṣabbarkum* 'There is no power and no strength save in God, may our Lord have mercy on him and forgive him, and make his abode heaven, and give you patience'.

(202) *lā ḥawl wa lā quwwa illa bi ḷḷāh, inna li ḷḷāhi wa inna ilayhi ragi'ūn, rabbina yirḥamha wi yiġfir laha wi yiskinha fasīḥ gannitu* 'There is no power and no

[27] Abu Gahl, 'Amr ibn Hishām al-Maḫzumi – a pagan leader from Quraysh and an opponent of the prophet Muhammad.

strength save in God, verily to God we belong and unto him is our return, may God have mercy on her and forgive her, and make her live in his vastest paradise'.

(203) *lā ilāha illa ḷḷāh, al-baqā' li llāh rabbina yirḥamha yiġfir laha wi yiskinha l-fardūs wi yiṣabbar ahlaha* 'There is no deity but God, only God is eternal, may our Lord have mercy on her and forgive her, and make her live in paradise, and give her family patience'.

All the material presented in this chapter is characterised by a high degree of formulaicity on various levels, which will be discussed in more detail in the following chapter. Another feature are multi-formulaic slots, observed especially in the comments made by people from the close environment of the mourner (204–205). An example of multi-formula expressions are prayers quoted verbatim or with modifications, although these were marked as atypical examples (206):

(204) *yiskinha fasīḥ gannitu wi yig'al 'abraha rawḍa min riyāḍ il-ganna* 'May [God] make her live in his vastest paradise and make her grave a garden from the gardens of paradise'.

(205) *yisabbitha 'and is-su'āl wi yig'al 'abraha rawḍa min riyāḍ il-ganna wi yiskinha gannit il-fardūs il-a'la* 'May [God] make her strong when she is asked [by the angels] and make her grave a garden from the gardens of paradise'.

(206) *aḷḷāhumma ġsilhā bi l-mā'i wa ṯalǧi wa l-bardi, aḷḷāhumma adḫilhā bi raḥmatika fī 'ibādika ṣ-ṣāliḥīna allaḏīna lā ḫawfa 'alayhim wa lā hum yaḥzinūna wa innā li ḷḷāhi wa innā ilayhi rāǧi'ūna wa l-biqā'u wa d-dawāmu li llāhi* 'Oh, God, wash her with water, snow and hail, oh God, grant her, with your mercy, entrance among your righteous servants, on whom "there is no fear, nor shall they grieve"[28], and verily to God we belong and unto him is our return, and the eternity and perpetuity belong to God'.

Some of the formulae taken from Muslim religious are rare and unconventional in their function played in the material. At the same time most of them are strongly formulaic and known to the average language user.

(207) *yi'nisu fi waḥšit 'abru wi yimidd baṣaru* 'May [God] make him feel comfortable in his grave and extend his eyesight'.

(208) *ahširha ma' aṣ-ṣadīqīna wa š-šuhadā' wa ḥusn ulā'ika rafīqan* 'Make her join the friends and the martyrs, and excellent are those as companions'.

(209) *yarfa' manzilataha min al-ǧanna* 'May [God] elevate her position in heaven'.

(210) *li ḷḷāhi mā a'ṭā wa li ḷḷāhi mā aḫaḏa* 'Whatever God takes is for him and whatever he gives, is for him'.

[28] Q10:62, translation: Yusuf Ali.

A slightly different group consists of comments commemorating the deceased, e.g., on the anniversary of their death. They are of a similar nature, although usually less formulaic, while there are more personal statements, memories and accounts. A characteristic formula in this group is (211) appearing 6 times:
(211) *tʿīš wi tiftikir* 'Live and remember'.

In the material, examples that are nonformulaic but take the form of blessings can be found.
(212) *yuzīḥ ʿannā hāḏā l-wibāʾ yā rabb* 'May [he] take away from us this epidemic, oh, Lord'[29].

The phrases *taqabbal* 'accept' and *amīn* 'amen' are usually used in response to condolences, but in the material, they sometimes appeared as a link between comments on the same post. In this case they were located at the beginning of the comment:
(213) *taqabbal wi yigʿalu fi mizān ḥasanatha* '[May God] accept and may [God] add it to the account of her good deeds'.
(214) *aḷḷāhumma amīn aḷḷāhumma taqabbal wi igʿalu fi mizān ḥasanatha* 'Oh, God, amen, oh, God, accept, and may [God] add it to the account of her good deeds'.

In the material, 228 examples do not have the core part. Of these, 37 are comments that contain only the opening formula or the framing formula, or both. There are also examples with two framing formulae.
(215) *la ilāha illā ḷḷāh* 'There is no deity but God'.
(216) *al-baqāʾ li llāh* 'Only God is eternal'.
(217) *al-baqāʾ li llāh, inna li ḷḷāhi wa inna ilayhi ragiʿūn* 'Only God is eternal, verily to God we belong and unto him is our return'.
(218) *lā ḥawl wa lā quwwa illa bi ḷḷāh* 'There is no power and no strength save in God'.
(219) *il-baʾiya fi ḥayātik* 'I am sorry for your loss [the rest is in your life]'.

21 other examples contain only the formulae (220) or (221).
(220) *ḥasbi ḷḷāh wa niʿma l-wakīl* 'God is sufficient for me and he is the best disposer of affairs'.
(221) *ḥasbina ḷḷāh wa niʿma l-wakīl* 'God is sufficient for me and he is the best disposer of affairs'.

The material also includes two examples containing only supplement II and one containing supplement I and II. 57 examples are religious formulae, curses, and

[29] The sentence refers to the global pandemic of SARS COV-2 (2020 and 2021).

spontaneous types of statements made as comments to the special case described earlier:

(222) *ya 'albi* 'Oh, my God, [my heart]!'

(223) *ya 'albi, ēh il ḥuzn wi l-waga' da?* 'Oh, my God! What a pain and sadness!'

Other examples include religious formulae used in an unconventional way – flowery and solemn supplications for mercy for the deceased, linguistically sophisticated consolations for the mourner, excerpts from prayers, verses from the Quran and Hadith. Between the slots discourse markers are used. They form a closed group of several pragmatically diverse expressions, which include:

- personal names (of the mourner and of the deceased),
- terms of address,
- terms of endearment,
- invocation *ya rabb* 'oh, God', *ya rabb il-'alamīn* 'oh, God of the worlds',
- *amīn* 'amen',
- *in šā' aḻḻāh* 'God willing'.

The use of invocations to God adds emphasis: *ya rabb* 'oh, Lord', *aḻḻāhumma* 'oh, God'. The blessing may be conveyed directly to the deceased:

(224) *alf raḥma wi nūr 'alēk ya 'amm maḥmūd* '[A thousand] mercy and light on you, uncle Mahmud'.

A direct address to the deceased as in: *ya 'amm ḥasan* 'oh, uncle Hasan', *'amm maḥmūd* 'uncle Mahmud' seems to serve underlining the fact that the one who died was close to the speaker and thus expresses solidarity with their family. Personal names and terms of endearment appear most frequently between opening or framing formula and core. A separate group consists of a few examples of *ya rabb* 'oh, Lord' followed by core I without an explicitly expressed subject.

Between the two slots of core, the phrase *ya rabb* constitutes the vast majority of DMs. Also, several examples of proper names and terms of endearment (mainly *ḥabībi/ḥabibti* 'my dear') and one term of address appear. Discourse markers between the core and the supplement are very rare and include some examples of *ya rabb* and some proper names with the vocative particle *ya*. Between supplement I and II DMs appear most often in the form of the invocations *ya rabb* 'oh, Lord', *ya rabb il-'alamīn* 'oh, Lord of the worlds'. Additionally, *amīn* 'amen', *aḻḻāhumma amīn* 'oh, God, amen' are frequent and the phrase *in šā' aḻḻāh* 'God willing' appears once. At the end of the sequence of formulae all kinds of DMs are possible. However, no discourse markers are allowed between the opening and framing formula.

In addition to formulae, the material studied also includes non-formulaic data, often without any reference to religion. They are usually a kind of comment added to a condolence, but sometimes appear independently. Due to the nature of such linguistic data, no structural types can be distinguished here. Thematically, they treat the subject of death in a number of different ways. Among them, several groups can be distinguished:

a) expressing concern for the mourner:
(225) *ḫalli bālik min nafsik* 'Take care of yourself'.

b) expressing compassion and solidarity:
(226) *ḥassa bīki waḷḷāhi l-ʿaẓīm* 'I know how you feel, really'.
(227) *rabbina maʿāk* 'May our Lord be with you'.
(228) *abkaytīni* 'You made me cry'.

c) glorifying the deceased:
(229) *waḷḷāhi kānit insāna gamīla wi aṣīla* 'She was really a beautiful and noble person'.
(230) *malāk wi makānu maʿa l-malayka* 'Angel whose place is among angels'.
(231) *aṭyab wi aḥann ab* 'The kindest and most affectionate father'.
(232) *kunti insāna ḫalūʾa wi muhazzaba* 'You were a virtuous and polite person'.

d) complementing the mourner:
(233) *ʾamar ma šāʾ aḷḷāh ʿalēki* 'Oh, my God, how gorgeous you are'.
(234) *iṣ-ṣūra gamīla winti gamīla ʾawi* 'The picture is beautiful and you are beautiful'.

e) remembering the deceased:
(235) *ʿala ṭūl fakra wi badʿīlu* 'I still remember and pray for him'.
(236) *kān nifsi ašufha ʾawi ʾabl ma timši* 'I wanted to see her before she's gone'.

f) expressing pain after the loss:
(237) *ʾaṭaʿti ʾalbi* 'My heart is aching'.
(238) *fiʿlan il-ḥuzn byimawwit* 'Really, too sad for words'.
(239) *waggaʿti ʾalbi* 'You made my heart ache'.

g) reminding of divine justice:
(240) *miš hayirūḥ kullu ʿand aḷḷāh* 'God will not forget about it'.
(241) *rabbina hayiruddilha ḥaʾʾaha in šāʾ aḷḷāh* 'God will give her justice, God willing'.
(242) *inti ʿand il-aḥann wi akīd hayigiblik ḥaʾʾik* 'You are now with the most affectionate [one] and he will surely give you justice'.

h) reassuring that the deceased is in paradise:
(243) *huwwa fi ʿālam agmal min ʿalamna masafāt* 'He is in a world way better than our world'.

(244) *huwwa akīd fi makān afḍal* 'He is surely in a better place'.
(245) *rabbina iḫtāru li yikūn ma'āh* 'Our Lord chose him to be with him'.

i) relating to the memory:
(246) *yimūt il-gasad wi tib'a ir-rūḥ ḥayya fi 'ulubna* 'The body dies and the soul remains alive in our hearts'.
(247) *aḥibba'na yiẓillu aḥyā li l-abad ṭalama mazālu fi 'ulubna wi 'u'ulna* 'Our loved ones remain alive as long as they are in our hearts and our minds'.

Additionally, there are many comments that cannot be grouped in terms of content. The total percentage of novel language in the material is only around 3% if we take a single sentence or its functional equivalent as a unit. The analysis carried out here shows that the comments posted in reaction to death announcements are largely formulaic and use a number of fixed religious expressions, most of which can be summarised in the general framework presented in Table 1.

7. Qualitative analysis of death announcements, comments containing condolences and their responses

The following qualitative analysis aims to discuss selected aspects of the formulaicity in utterances related to the subject of death in three different communicative types: death announcements, comments, and dialogues. In this part, the material from two periods will be analysed. The majority will consist of data obtained for the purposes of this work including 20 death announcements, 857 comments and 220 responses to comments from 2020–2021. On the other hand, a corpus of Facebook conversations of 60 people from 2007–2014 was also used, previously analysed in 2016 in my doctoral thesis *Linguistic Etiquette and Taboo in the Language of Young Egyptians. A Text-Based Study of Online Communication*. What is of key importance for the current study is more or less conventional formulae, as presented in the previous chapter. All of the analysed comments appeared in reaction to a death announcement. In this chapter, the bulk of the formulae will be extended to include posts and dialogues.

7.1. Death announcements

This analysis encompasses death announcements appearing on Facebook in the form of posts. Most of them concerned the death of a speaker's loved one that happened shortly before the publication of the post. Some of them, however, related to situations that took place in the past, e.g., appeared on the anniversary of the death. Therefore, the tabooisation of the theme may have faded for the speaker, to some extent, over the passage of time. These posts refer to a tragedy that has already been processed. The pain that the authors indicate is more conscious and is talked about more openly. There are fewer prayers and more poetic attempts, although of course this observation is anecdotal rather than hard fact, taking into account the fact that the material analysed here is limited in size.

The material analysed here consists of 20 death announcements of differing lengths. A single sentence or its functional equivalent is assumed as a unit. Announcements consist of 16 sentences on average, although the differences are significant. Two of the announcements consists of a single sentence, while the longest one has 70 sentences. The material was randomly selected form enormous amount of such data available on Facebook. The most surprising feature turned out to be its diversity. The entire material contains 323 sentences, of which the conventional formulae discussed in the previous chapter constitute just over 15% (49 formulae). Four announcements do not contain any formula at all whereas four examples are fully formulaic (these are short announcements of 1–10 sentences).

Death announcements appearing here have little similarity with obituaries. They are more spontaneous and do not have a regular form. Some resemble, to some extent, oral utterances, and largely reflect the individual character of the people who publish them. They differ in terms of the relation between the author and the deceased – the relationships included family members, e.g. father, grandmother, uncle, and in these, the expressions of pain dominate. If the deceased was a friend of the author, there are more memories of moments spent together or, for instance reflecting on the enormity of injustice in the world (in the case of young deceased). They include among other things a poem written in the first person and addressed to the deceased, as well as various more or less poetic attempts (249). Frequent repetition both on the level of the utterance as well as the interaction, e.g., *ya rabb hawwin, ya rabb hawwin, ya rabb hawwin* 'oh, Lord, make it easier, oh, Lord, make it easier, oh, Lord, make it easier' turn the utterance into a half poetic, half magical invocation that can be single or multi-authored, composed of blessings or pieces of *du'ā'* 'prayer'. In this way, a single act of speech is turned into an event of a supernatural and mystical character. In the example below we can see how the sequences of repetition follow each other to give the effect of a litany. Fragments of prayers for the deceased (usually spontaneously selected formulae) are cited (250), as well as Hadiths:

(248) *innā li ḷḷāhi wa innā ilayhi rāǧiʻūna, tuwuffiya ilā raḥmati ḷḷāh rāmi fī hudūʼin wa salāmin, baʻd iṣābatihi bi l-maraḍi l-ḫabīṯ allaḏī ʼaṣābahu faǧaʼatan min hawālay šahrin wa n-niṣf baʻda ʼan kāna miṯālan li n-našāṭi wa l-ḥayawiyyati wa quwwati l-ǧism, māta bi maraḍin ḫaṭīrin fī baṭnihi wa kāna mawtuhu bi hudūʼin wa huwa nāʼim, wa lam yašʻur bihi man kānū bi ǧiwārihi wa lam yuktašaf mawtuhu ʼillā baʻda ʼarbaʻi sāʻātin wa hāḏā dalīlu riḍāʼi ḷḷāhi ʻanhu* 'Verily to God we belong and unto him is our return, Rāmi passed away,

in calmness and peace, after he was afflicted by a malicious disease that befell him unexpectedly about month and a half ago, after he had been an example of health, vitality and physical powers. He died from a dangerous illness in his stomach and his death was peaceful, in his sleep. Those who were gathered around him didn't even notice it, his death was discovered four hours later, which is a sign of God's satisfaction with him'.

(249) *aḷḷāhumma innī lā as'aluka radda l-qaḍā'i wa lakinnī as'aluka l-luṭfa fīhi, aḷḷāhumma innī lā as'aluka radda l-qaḍā'i wa lakinnī as'aluka l-luṭfa fīhi, aḷḷāhumma innī lā as'aluka radda l-qaḍā'i wa lakinnī as'aluka l-luṭfa fīhi, aḷḷāhumma anta waḥdaka ta'limu ḥağma l-'alami fa yā rabb hawwin, yā rabb hawwin, yā rabb hawwin, yā rabb hawwin, yā rabb hawwin, yā rabb hawwin, aḷḷāhumma anta waḥdaka ta'limu kam kuntu uḥibbuhu fa ġfir lahu qadra ḥubbī lahu, yā rabb hawwin, yā rabb hawwin, yā rabb hawwin, yā rabb hawwin, yā rabb hawwin, yā rabb hawwin, yā rabb hawwinn* 'Oh, God, I don't ask you to change your verdict but I ask you for kindness for him. Oh, God, I don't ask you to change your verdict but I ask you for kindness for him. Oh, God, I don't ask you to change your verdict but I ask you for kindness for him. Oh, God, only you know how big is my pain, so please Lord, make it easier, please Lord, make it easier, please Lord, make it easier, please Lord, make it easier, please Lord, make it easier, please Lord, make it easier. Oh, God, only you know how much I loved him, so forgive him with the amount of forgiveness equal to my love for him. Please Lord, make it easier, please Lord, make it easier, please Lord, make it easier, please Lord, make it easier, please Lord, make it easier, please Lord, make it easier!'

(250) *aḷḷāhumma ġfir lahu wa rḥamhu, aḷḷāhumma tağāwaz 'an say'ātihi, aḷḷāhumma akṯir min ḥasanātihi, aḷḷāhumma akrim nuzulahu, aḷḷāhumma wassi' mudḫalahu, aḷḷāhumma abdilhu dāran ḫayran min dārihi wa ahlan ḫayran min ahlihi, aḷḷāhumma ğāfi l-arḍa 'an ğānibayhi, aḷḷāhumma ġsilhu bi l-mā'i wa ṯ-ṯalği wa l-bard, aḷḷāhumma naqihi mina ḏ-ḏunūb wa l-ḫaṭāyā kamā yunaqqā ṯ-ṯawbu l-abyaḍ mina d-danas*[30] 'Oh, God, forgive him and have mercy on him. Oh, God, forgive his sins and multiply his good deeds. Oh, God, make his resting place a noble one. Oh, God, facilitate his entry. Oh, God, give him in exchange a home better than his home [on earth] and a family better than his family. Oh, God, keep the earth away from his two sides. Oh, God, wash him with water, snow and hail. Oh, God, purify him from sins as a white garment is cleansed of dirt'.

In some cases, asking for prayers replaces direct information about death or suffering:

[30] Sunan Ibn Majah 1553, Book 6, Hadith 121. Translation based on: https://sunnah.com/ibnmajah:1553, access: April 2021.

(251) *tid'ilna kida* 'Pray for us'.
(252) *ṭūl manti bitid'i lilli māt akīd rabbina hayisaḫḫarlik ḥadd yid'īlik barḍu* 'As long as you pray for those who died, surely God will give you someone to pray for you'.
(253) *as'alukum ad-du'ā' li ḫāli* 'I ask you to pray for my uncle'.

One of the announcements offers gratitude for many condolences the mourner obtained through other media, (in person or by phone), it is also accompanied by a request for prayer. This way, the author is freed from the burden of formulating the narration about her relative's death:
(254) *šukran li kull man taqaddam lanā bi l-'izā' fī wālidī, as'alukum ad-du'ā'a lahu* 'Thanks to everyone who condoled us after my father's death, I ask you to pray for him'.

In another example, the author refers to the posts previously published by friends of the deceased person, so instead of the typical announcement of death, she expresses her thanks.
(255) *rabbina yataqabbalu minkum ǧamī'an wa yazīdukum aḍ'āfa muḍā'afātin mina l-ḥasanāt* 'May our Lord accept all [of your prayers] and multiply your good deeds many times over'.

The following example is the closest to the textual form of obituaries. It is written in MSA. It contains information about death given directly, albeit using the euphemistic verb *tuwuffiya* 'pass away' in place of the more tabooed *māta* 'die'. Includes a request to pray for mercy and forgiveness for the deceased and ends with a closing formula *lā ḥawl wa lā quwwa illa bi ḷḷāh* 'there is no power and no strength save in God' – a more general expression referring to tragedies befalling man in life, the magnitude of which is beyond their strength. For a Muslim, submission to the power of God almighty makes a person feel grounded and secure. This fragment is deeply formulaic on many levels, especially conceptual. It shows the ordering of thoughts according to the classic model of expression in such situations. It refers to a repetitive life situation enshrined in a specific ritual without, resorting to conventional formulae used in such cases.
(256) *tuwuffiyat 'ilā raḥmati ḷḷāh 'ammatī, ar-raǧā'a ad-du'ā'a lahā bi r-raḥmati wa l-maġfarati wa ṯ-ṯabāti 'inda s-su'āl, lā ḥawla wa lā quwwata illā bi ḷḷāh* 'My aunt passed away to the mercy of God, I ask for your prayers for [God's] mercy and forgiveness and to strengthen her when she's questioned [by the angels]. There is no power and no strength save in God'.

As for the scope of the formulae appearing in the material, they include the supplications identified in the previous chapter as the core, in particular core I:

(257) *aḷḷāintaqalahh yirḥamha wi yiġfir laha* 'May God have mercy on her and forgive her'.
(258) *aḷḷāh yirḥamak ya ʿamm ḥasan* 'May God have mercy on you, uncle Hasan'.
(259) *aḷḷāh yirḥamik ya umniyya wi yiġfirlik wi tkūni min ahl il-fardūs il-aʿla ya rabb amīn* 'May God have mercy on you, Omnia, and forgive you and may you be one of the dwellers of the greatest garden, oh, Lord, amen'.

Example (259) implements the scheme in a broader scope, the full two-part version of the core and supplement I occurs. Address terms including the deceased's name *ya umniyya* and a phrase addressed to God – *ya rabb amīn* 'oh, Lord, amen' are used. In another example, a male speaker asks God for forgiveness for himself (first) and for his deceased father. This example interestingly illustrates the Muslim way of looking at life as a stage along the road to eternity, as well as the awareness of one's own sinfulness and the need for a future account of the sins of life.
(260) *rabbi ġfir liyya wi li waldi* 'Lord, forgive me and my father'.

Several times the formula *ḥasbi ḷḷāh wa niʿma l-wakīl* appears in posts relating to the special case discussed earlier.

The above information is not to imply that in the rest of the material novel language is used. Although, in fact, most of the sentences are non-formulaic in nature, various idiomatic expressions, collocations, politeness formulae, discourse markers appear, though rarely. Often, other types of religious formulae are used, not necessarily closely related to the subject of death, e.g. each time the name of a prophet or the word "prophet" is mentioned, it is followed by a formula common in the whole Muslim world *ṣallā ḷḷāhu ʿalayhi wa sallam* usually translated as 'peace be upon him'. The phrase (261) below is also formulaic, it is used to introduce a fragment quoted from the Quran or Hadith:
(261) *qāla rasūlu ḷḷāh ṣallā aḷḷāhu ʿalayhi wa sallam* 'said the prophet of God, peace be upon him'.

Example (262) shows a similar situation. A formulaic term of endearment was used by the mourner as a proof of her deceased grandmother's tenderness, who used to refer to her in this metaphorical way.
(262) *ya nūr ʿīni* 'My love [the light of my eye]'.

Another example illustrates collocations and the conventional use of language forms. First of all, the expression *naṣibha inn...* 'her fate is that/to' illustrates the Muslim way of looking at human life as an account of a divine plan over which man has no influence. The phrase *naṣib* 'fate' has a number of synonyms in Arabic, but the convention dictates that only this one sounds natural in this situation. In the example below, another collocation is seen *ḥaṣalit muškila bēn ... wi bēn ...* 'a problem occurred between ... and ...' Only formulaic considerations make this expression more natural in this context than, e.g., *ḥaṣalit ṣuʿūba bēn... wi bēn...* 'a difficulty occurred between ... and...' Secondly, the expression *li l-asaf* 'unfortunately', like the previous ones, could be replaced, e.g., by *li l-ḥuzn* 'sadly', but then it would lose its naturalness:

(263) *naṣibha li l-asaf inn ḥaṣalit muškila binha wi bēn guzha* 'It happened [it was her fate] that a problem occurred between her and her husband'.

In each of the following cases, the use determines the connectivity of the expression components.

(264) *ʿala ṭūl* 'All the time'.
(265) *āh waḷḷāh* 'Yes, I swear'.
(266) *laʿalla wa ʿasā* 'Maybe'.

Another example is the construct *ēh* 'what' + open class element + *da/di* 'this' that functions as an expressive. In the collection of death announcements examined here, they appear several times:

(267) *ēh kammiyit il-qahr wi wagaʿ il-ʾalb da?* 'What a pain and oppression!'
(268) *ēh ʿadam it-tarbiya aw id-dīn aw il-aḫlāʾ aw iḍ-ḍamīr da?* 'What a lack of manners! No religion, no morals, no conscience at all!'
(269) *ēh il-ʾaraf da?* 'What a disgust!'

A slightly different type of formulaicity is represented by the next two examples. In the first case, there is a phenomenon discussed by Wray (2002) that could be described as "conceptual formulaicity". It seems that the idea of a beloved one departing forever is unbearable; therefore, the human psyche, supported by religious faith, prefers to think of it as something temporary, which at some point will lead to another meeting. The author of the sentence below reverses the formulaic character of the farewell formula *ilā liqāʾ* 'see you' in order to return to the literal message contained in it about the next meeting ("until we see each other"). However, the same idea and the same stylistic measure can be found in other languages with phrases such as "see you," "goodbye". In Arabic, this can be realised in various expressive ways, because this is not a lexical form or grammatical structure, but the idea itself, which is recurrent:

(270) *lan aqūla widāʿan bal aqūlu ilā liqāʾ liqāʾin ǧamīl in šāʾ aḷḷāh* 'I will not say "farewell", I will say "till I see you again, till I see you happily", God willing'.
(271) *ḥasbi ḷḷāh wa niʿma l-wakīl fi kulli ẓālim* 'God is sufficient for me and he is the best disposer of affairs against every oppressor'.

Another example of conceptual formulaicity is the use of generalisations with *kull* 'every' after the formula *ḥasbi ḷḷāh wa niʿma l-wakīl* 'God is sufficient for me and he is the best disposer of affairs' in expressions relating to the special case. It does not always occur; sometimes there is a direct reference to the specific situation, e.g. *ḥasbi ḷḷāh wi ni'ma l-wakīl fi guzha* 'God is sufficient for me and he is the best disposer of affairs against her husband', although the mere frequency of examples containing *kull* 'every' suggests that the idea behind it is repetitive.

Nevertheless, the above examples of formulaic expressions in their majority do not constitute a part of discourse on death; unlike the previously analysed formulae, they may be used in a variety of contexts. Therefore, in the following part of discussion, I will only consider formulae in the full sense of the word.

Before we proceed to other types of material, one interesting issue should be noted. Researchers report that traditionally obituaries avoid naming death and use various euphemistic techniques. Al-Khatib and Salem (2011) say Jordanian obituaries resort to euphemisms while invoking "death". They found that 62% of the obituaries they studied used the expression *intaqalah ʔila raħmatellah* 'moved to the mercy of God' and 34% – the expression *waafat'hu ʔl-maneyyah* 'death came to him', meaning 'he passed away'. Other examples were only occasional, e.g., *intaqalah ʔila ʔl-ʔmjaad as- samaaweyyah* 'moved to the glory of God' – 2%, 'moved to the neighbourhood of his Lord' – 1%. The authors found only three examples of direct word or expression relating to death (*mawt, wafāt*) and one relating to dying (*tuwuffi*). In the material analysed here, apart from those described above, there are relatively frequent direct references to death. The verb *māt* 'die' appears in 6 out of 20 analysed posts. It should be added here, however, that 5 of these posts concerned the death of friends, and only one post announced the death of a family member – a grandmother:

(272) *innaha mātit wi hiyya nifsana tšūf awladha* 'She died while she was longing to see her children'.
(273) *wi mātit min al-qahra* 'She died from oppression'.
(274) *mātit, āh waḷḷāhi mātit, mātit ṣaḥbiti* 'She died, she really died, my friend died'.
(275) *gidditi il-ḥabība mātit* 'My beloved grandmother died'.

The verb *tuwuffiya* or the dialectal *itwaffa* 'to pass away' is much milder in its expressiveness and perceived as a more noble term. In the analysed material, both versions appear several times:

(276) *tuwuffiyat 'ilā raḥmati ḷḷāh* 'She passed away to the glory of God'.
(277) *itwaffit miš 'arfa izzāyy* 'She passed away, I don't know how'.
(278) *itwaffit fi 'izz šababha* 'She passed away in the prime of life'.

Even more indirect are statements such as: *rāh/rāḥit is-sama* 'went do heaven', appearing in what seems to be a Muslim-Christian death announcement. However, when it comes to the noun "death", the word *mawt* (*mōt*) does not appear once, but in some posts, it is replaced by the softer word *wafāt*.

(279) *aḏ-ḏikrā s-sanawiyyatu l-ūlā li wafāti ǧaddatī l-ḥabība* 'The first anniversary of the death of my beloved grandmother'.

(280) *ḫabar wafatha bi n-nisbāli kān ṣaʿb giddan giddan* 'The information about her death was very hard for me'.

7.2. Comments and dialogues

While consoling a person in grief, usually positive politeness strategies, such as using in-group identity markers, asserting common ground and the expressions of empathy are used to soothe and offer comfort. Blessing for the deceased often comes in the form of assurance, which might have an intensifying effect:

(281) *rāḥit li makān aḥsan* 'She went to a better place'.

(282) *tkūn fi makān agmal wi aḥla wi aḥsan min hina* 'May she be in a place that is more beautiful, prettier and better than here'.

It happens that they are intensified by the repetition of *agmal* 'more beautiful', *aḥla* 'prettier', *aḥsan* 'better', which is probably to impress on the recipient of the message that there is no doubt about the deceased person being in heaven. Intensifiers are used along with the blessings:

(283) *aḷḷāhumma rḥamu raḥma wasʾa* 'Oh, God, have great mercy on him' (*muṭlaq* construction).

Condolences in the material give the impression of an intense emotional load. Also, DM slots appear between crucial elements of utterances, e.g., invocations to God, adding emphasis:

(284) *ya rabb* 'Oh, Lord'.

(285) *aḷḷāhumma* 'Oh, God'.

(286) *in šāʾ aḷḷāh* 'God willing'.

In the previous chapter, 857 comments containing condolences were analysed. A certain pattern can be distinguished, in which the main parts (formulae) appear in a regular order. This pattern is followed by speakers in the community to differing degrees. Thus, two types of expressions typically placed at the beginning were found: the opening formula is one referring generally to religion and to God's omnipotence (*ḥawqala* and other conventionalised forms are used). The framing formula introduces the theme of death (for instance "the supplication in times of hardship"). They are followed by an element referred to as the core, which is a two-part structure. The first part is usually a supplication for mercy, while the second is for forgiveness. The first of these elements appears in the vast majority of comments, even very short ones. Then comes another element, referred to as the supplement that aims to bless the deceased in its first part and the mourner in its second part. Supplement II – a comforting formulae addressed to the family and relatives of the deceased is slightly less often. After such a set of formulae, a blessing directed to the entire Muslim community (287) might appear:

(287) *rabbina yirḥam amwāt il-muslimīn* 'God have mercy on the deceased Muslims'.

The blessing in the core or supplement may be conveyed directly to the deceased:

(288) *alf raḥma wi nūr ʿalēk ya ʿamm maḥmūd* '[A thousand] mercy and light on you, uncle Mahmud'.

Usually, this set of formulae ends with personal comments, words of comfort and compliments addressed to the mourner. They are either non-formulaic in nature or contain various elements of the right hemispheric language, normally present in any text and not directly related to the theme of death, and therefore, they will not be further analysed. A few examples in which both Muslims and Christians comment are unique in the material are listed below:

(289) (a) *aḷḷāh yirḥamak ya ʿamm ḥasan* 'May God have mercy on you, uncle Ḥasan'.
(b) *subḥāna l-ḥayy allaḏi lā yamūt, aḷḷāh yirḥamak ya ʿamm ḥasan* 'Glory be to the living, who does not die. May God have mercy on you, uncle Ḥasan'.
(c) *inna li ḷḷāhi wa inna ilayhi ragiʿūn* 'Verily to God we belong and unto him is our return'.
(d) *al-biqā li ḷḷāh rabbina yigʿalha āḥir il-ʾaḥzān* 'Only God is eternal, May our Lord make it the last of [your] sorrows'.

(290) (a) *šukran li kull man taqaddama lanā bi l-ʿizāʾ fī wālidī, asʾalukum ad-duʿāʾa lahu* 'Thanks to everyone who condoled us after my father's death, I ask you to pray for him'.
(b) *al-biqāʾ li ḷḷāh wa atamannā min aḷḷāh an yunʿima ʿalayka bi l-ǧannati wa l-ʿatqi min an-nār* 'Only God is eternal, I hope God will let you enjoy heaven and release you from the fire'.
(c) *aḷḷāhumma ġfir lahu wa rḥamhu wa adḫilhu fasīḥa ǧannatika yā arḥama r-raḥīmīn wa ǧʿalhu yā rabb min ʿutaqāʾa šahri ramaḍān, yā rabb* 'Oh, God, forgive his sins and have mercy on him and let him into your vastest heaven, the most merciful, and let him, oh Lord, among those who are freed in the month of Ramadan, oh, Lord'.
(d) *aḷḷāh yirḥamu wi yigʿal maswāh il-ganna* 'May God have mercy on him and make his abode heaven'.

7.3. Response to the condoler

The acceptance of condolences and words of comfort is often communicated by (291), often accompanied by *aḷḷāhumma* 'oh, God' as in (292) or the invocation *ya rabb* 'oh, Lord' (293). Finally, all of those forms might be used together (294):

(291) *amīn* 'Amen'.
(292) *aḷḷāhumma amīn* 'Oh, God, amen'.
(293) *amīn ya rabb* 'Amen, oh, God'.
(294) *aḷḷāhumma amīn ya rabb il-ʿalamīn* 'Oh, Lord, amen, oh, Lord of the worlds'.

Instead of this, the following expression might be used, though less frequently:

(295) *rabbina yataqabbal* 'May our Lord accept'.
(296) *yataqabbal minkum ad-duʿāʾ* 'May [God] accept your prayer'.
(297) *rabbina yataqabbal minkum ad-duʿāʾ* 'May our Lord accept your prayer'.

Very rarely all of these are used at once, such as in the following example, along with a term of address or endearment:

(298) *aḷḷāhumma amīn ya rabb il-ʿalamīn, rabbina yataqabbal duʿāʾik ya ṭanṭ* 'Oh, God, amen, oh, Lord of the worlds. May our Lord accept your prayer, auntie'.
(299) *rabbina yataqabbal minnik ad-duʿāʾ ya rabb ḥabibti* 'May our Lord accept your prayer, oh, Lord, my dear'.

Other expressions are also used, albeit rarely:

(300) *gazākum aḷḷāh ḫayran* 'May God reward you well'.
(301) *amīn amīn amīn gazākum aḷḷāh gamīʿan kull il-ḫayr wi gaʿal duʿākum fi mizankum* 'Amen, amen, amen, may God reward you all well and add your prayers to the account of your good deeds'.
(302) *rabbina yiḫallīki ya rabb ya ṭanṭ* 'May our Lord keep you safe, auntie'.

Terms of address including professional and other titles, names, honorifics and terms of endearment are found in abundance:

(303) *aḷḷāhumma amīn ya duktūr* 'Oh, God, amen, doctor'.
(304) *yataqabbal duʿāʾik ḥabibti* 'May [God] accept your prayer, my dear'.

In the material analysed, dialogues consisting in short exchanges are highly schematic. We distinguish between three types of sequences containing condolences along with their prescribed responses. Most of the comments stand alone, i.e., they are not followed by any kind of answer. However, in this particular portion of the material, a group of condolences that triggered answers on the part of the mourner was selected (counting 220 turns). The sequences were of three types: duplets, triplets and very rarely quadruplets. Most of the answers were very specific and did not entail much variation. Duplets usually involve *amīn* 'amen' in the answer.

(305) (a) *aḷḷāh yirḥamu ḥabībi* 'May God have mercy on him, my dear'.
(b) *aḷḷāhumma amīn ya rabb rabbina yiḫallīk* 'Oh, God, amen, oh, Lord, may our Lord keep you safe'.

(306) (a) *rabbina yirḥamu wi yiġfirlu wi yiṣabbarkum* 'May our Lord have mercy on him and forgive him, and give you patience'.
(b) *aḷḷāhumma amīn ya rabb naglā rabbina yiḫallīki wi yataqabbal minnik id-duʿā* 'Oh, God, amen, oh, Lord, Nagla, may our Lord keep you safe and accept your prayer'.

The condoled person may express thanks by blessing the speaker. He/she may as well answer many comments with one response, where example (310) depicts the complete conversation involving four interactants:

(307) *gazākum aḷḷāh gamīʿan kull il-ḫayr wi gaʿal duʿākum fi mizankum* 'May God reward all of you with his goodness, and consider your prayers on the day of judgment'.

(308) *yiḫallīki liyya wi yibarikli fīki ya rabb* 'May [God] keep you safe for me and bless you, oh, God'.

(309) *ǧazākum aḷḷāh dāʾiman kull al-ḫayri wa mā ʾarākum šarran fī man tuḥibbūna ʾabadan* 'May God always reward you with the goodness and make you never see evil in who you love'.

(310) (a) *tuwuffiyat ʾilā raḥmati ḷḷāh ʿammatī, ar-raǧāʾa ad-duʿāʾa lahā bi r-raḥmati wa l-maġfarati wa ṯ-ṯabāti ʿinda s-suʾāl, lā ḥawla wa lā quwwata illā bi ḷḷāh* 'My aunt passed away to the mercy of God, I ask for your prayers for [God's] mercy and forgiveness and to strengthen her when she's questioned [by the angels]. There is no power and no strength save in God'.
(b) *al-baqāʾ li ḷḷāh, rabbina yirḥamha wi yiġfirlaha wi yiṣabbarku* 'Only God is eternal. May our Lord have mercy for her and forgive her and give you patience'.
(c) *lā ḥawl wa lā quwwa illa bi ḷḷāh, inna li ḷḷāh wa inna ilayhi ragiʿūn, aḷḷāh yirḥamha wi yiṣabbarkum* 'There is no power and no strength save in God, verily to God we belong and unto him is our return, may God have mercy on her and give you patience'.
(d) *al-baqāʾ li ḷḷāh, aḷḷāhumma ṯabbithā ʿind as-suʾāl* 'Only God is eternal. Oh, God, keep her strong when she is asked [by the angels]'.
(a) *amīn amīn amīn gazākum aḷḷāh gamīʿan kull il-ḫayr wa gaʿal duʿākum fi mizankum* 'Amen, amen, amen, may God reward all of you with his goodness, an consider your prayers on the day of judgment'.

Triplets were the most common in the corpus. They entail a formula of condolences (a), the mourner's response (b), constructed around the word *amīn* 'amen', and the condoler's response as well, containing the verb *yataqabbal* 'accept' (a). Sometimes, additional blessings are given, especially in the third part of the sequence.

(311) (a) *rabbina yirḥamu wi yiskinu l-fardūs il-aʿla* 'May our Lord have mercy on him and make him live in the greatest garden'.
(b) *aḷḷāhumma amīn ya rabb* 'Oh, God, amen, oh, Lord'.
(a) *rabbina yataqabbal minnik id-duʿā ya rabb ḥabibti* 'May our Lord accept your prayer, oh, Lord, my dear'.

(312) (a) *rabbina yirḥamu wi yiġfirlu wi yiskinu fasīḥ gannitu* 'May our Lord have mercy on him and forgive him and make him live in his vastest paradise'.
(b) *aḷḷāhumma amīn ya rabb* 'Oh, God, amen, oh, Lord'.
(a) *rabbina yataqabbal minnik id-duʿā ya rabb wi yurzuʾik iṣ-ṣaḥḥa wi ṭūl ʿumr* 'May our Lord accept your prayer. Oh, Lord, and give you health and long life'.

(313) (a) *rabbina yirḥamu wi ġfirlu wi yiskinu fasīḥ gannitu* 'May our Lord have mercy on him and forgive him and make him live in his vastest paradise'.
(b) *aḷḷāhumma amīn ya rabb ḥabībi* 'Oh, God, amen, oh, Lord, my dear'.
(a) *rabbina yataqabbal minnik id-duʿā ya rabb wi yigazīki kull il-ḫēr dayman* 'May our Lord accept your prayer, oh, Lord, and reward you well'.

(314) (a) *rabbina yirḥamu wi yiṣabbarik* 'May Lord have mercy on him and give you patience'.
(b) *aḷḷāhumma amīn ya rabb il-ʿalamīn* 'Oh, God, amen, oh, Lord of the worlds'.
(a) *rabbina yiʿawwiḍik ʿannu ḫēr ya rabb* 'May our Lord compensate [him] for you well, oh, Lord'.

The last example contains a less conventional, but also to some extent recurrent answer form the condoler in the form of a blessing. Quadruplets are very rare in the material. The last part of the sequence is always an expression of submission to the will of God:

(315) (a) *rabbina yirḥamu raḥma wasʿa wi yiṣabbarik* 'May Lord have [great] mercy on him and give you patience'.
(b) *aḷḷāhumma amīn ya rabb* 'Oh, God, amen, oh Lord'.
(a) *rabbina yiʿawwiḍik ḫēr ya rabb* 'May our Lord compensate it for you well'.
(b) *il-ḥamdu li llāh ʿala kulli šīʿ* 'Praise be to God for everything'.

Repetition of *amīn* 'amen' occurs often in the material and it is felt to be more cordial and heartier than a single *amīn*.

(316) *amīn, amīn, amīn ya rabb il-ʿalamīn* 'Amen, amen, amen, oh, Lord of the worlds'.

7.4. Variability in formulae

There is no doubt that much of the material analysed in this work, published on the Internet in the context of the death taboo, is formulaic. This means that the same phrases appear in recurrent patterns in similar contexts. Sometimes, in the case of formulae, the context automates their usage so strongly that not only the referential meaning is significantly reduced, but also their form, a fact that has already been mentioned as a characteristic feature of formulae. This may be of a systemic nature or may manifest itself in the scheme of individual idiolects[31]. A formula found in October 2020 in a Polish profile on Facebook may serve as an example of this: *spoczywaj spokoju* 'rest, peace!' is a nonsensical sentence posted by a young man on the occasion of his brother's death, in place of the expected *spoczywaj w pokoju* 'rest in peace', derived from the phrase appearing in the Latin translation of the Psalms *requiescat in pace*. The possibility that this was a play of words was ruled out; therefore, the modification of the form of the expression was not intended by the author. The abbreviation can be explained in two ways. Perhaps the author wanted to say *spoczywaj w spokoju* 'rest in peace (calmness)' and a typing error occurred – the preposition was omitted. It is more likely, however, that the author inaccurately remembered the form of the fixed formula. Being used automatically, such formulae are applicable and appropriate in the context of death, thus they do not relate necessarily to their referential meaning. This is due to the fact that, as many researchers emphasise (e.g. Van Lancker Sidtis 2012a, 2012b), formulae are remembered and extracted whole from memory. However, this does not explain the minor or major modifications taking place within the formulae, observed in the vast majority of them. To provide an example, perhaps the most basic formula in the discussed material, playing the role of core I, takes the following forms (I list the majority of the examples here, but certainly not all possible combinations in which this formula appears):

(317) *aḷḷāh/rabbina yirḥamu/ha/hum* 'May God/our Lord have mercy on him/her/them'.

(318) *aḷḷāh/rabbina yirḥam* 'May God/our Lord have mercy on' + kinship term.

(319) *aḷḷāh/rabbina yirḥamak/ik/kum (ku)* 'May God/our Lord have mercy on you' (masculine/feminine/plural).

(320) *aḷḷāhumma/ya rabb irḥamu/ha/hum* 'Oh, God/oh, Lord, have mercy on him/her/them'.

---

[31] Although the relation between idiolects and formulae has not been well described so far, it can be assumed that since formulaic language is processed in the areas of brain responsible for the appreciation of context, pragmatic conditions, emotions and gestures, it is the experience of an individual that influences the use of formulae.

(321) *ya rabb yirḥamu/ya rabb yirḥamha/ya rabb yirḥamhum* 'Oh, Lord, may [he] have mercy on him/her/them'.
(322) *raḥamhu(u)/raḥamhā(ha)/raḥamhum aḷḷāh* 'May God have mercy on him/her/them'.

Kuiper and associates conclude that "idioms are both compositional and non-compositional at the same time, at different levels of processing" (2007: 324). The mechanism by which compositionality and noncompositionality are combined in idioms and (in a broader sense – formulae) has not been fully elucidated by researchers. An additional problem is that formulae vary significantly as to the extent to which they accept variability. There exist fixed formulae, one might say – functioning as single words withdrawn from the memory. They can be originally invariant expressions or fossilised in their fixed form despite their compositionality, as for instance the greeting *is-salamu alaykum* 'peace be upon you', where the 2nd person plural pronoun is fixed regardless of to whom the formula is directed (the same can be found in Ferguson 1997a).

Among fixed formulae, opening and framing formulae come to the fore. Both groups have a religious lineage and are used widely throughout the Arab Islamic world. The pragmatic scope of opening formulae is wider. They are not only used in relation to death, but in various life situations, usually when important events are happening or when strong emotions are involved, although this is not a necessary condition. These formulae are fixed in terms of their grammatical form, however, they are subject to intensification within a very strictly defined scheme, referring to the whole formula or its individual elements. *Ḥawqala* is intensified with *al-ʿalī al-ʿaẓīm* 'the highest, the greatest', whereas *lā ilāha illā ḷḷāh* 'there is no deity but God' – the formula of the Shahada is usually intensified by adding *waḥdu* 'only him' to *aḷḷāh*:
(323) *lā ḥawl wa lā quwwa illa bi ḷḷāh* 'There is no power and no strength save in God > *lā ḥawl wa lā quwwa illa bi ḷḷāhi l-ʿalī al-ʿaẓīm* 'There is no power and no strength save in God the highest, the greatest'.
(324) *lā ilāha illā ḷḷāh* 'there is no deity but God' > *lā ilāha illā ḷḷāh waḥdu* 'there is no deity but God, only him'.
(325) *aḷḷāhu akbar* 'God is the greatest'.

Framing formulae relate specifically to the situation of death, and just like the above, they are common in the entire Muslim Arab world. As for the first of them (355), it is a fragment of a Quranic surah and is always quoted in the same form. The latter, on the other hand, evokes discussion in Egyptian society, despite the fact that it appears more often in the analysed material than the former in the function of a framing formula. The controversy surrounding it is related to the parallel existence of widespread formulae *il-baʾiya fi ḥayātak* 'I am sorry for your loss [the rest is in your life]' and *ḥayātak il-ba'ya* 'may you live long [lit. your life is the remaining one]'. Modern metadiscourse tries to remove the former two from usage and replace them with *al-baqā' li llāh* 'only God is eternal'. This formula is, similarly to the previous ones, fixed, but it is possible to intensify it by adding the repetition *ad-dawām* 'perpetuity' or by adding *waḥdu* 'he alone' to *aḷḷāh*:

(326) *inna li llāh wa inna ilayhi ragi'ūn* 'Verily to God we belong and unto him is our return'.

(327) *al-baqā' li llāh* 'Only God is eternal' > *al-baqā' wa d-dawām li llāh* 'The eternity and perpetuity belong to God' > *al-baqā' li llāhi waḥdu* 'Only God is eternal, he alone' > *al-baqā' wa d-dawām li llāhi waḥdu* 'The eternity and perpetuity belong to God, only him'.

The fixed formulae include two more expressions used in everyday life that appear here at the end of blessings, as they seem to indicate humility and submission to God:

(328) *bi izni ḷḷāh* 'With God's permission'.

(329) *in šā' aḷḷāh* 'God willing'.

Wray (2002: 50) says "[s]ome variable sequences permit only a particular limited range of morphological possibilities (e.g., *it's been/it'll be/it's a devil of a job*)". Others, according to the author, accept a slight change in content words, she exemplifies this with "*a piece* or *slice of the action*; *show* or *teach SOMEONE* (or *know* or *learn*) *the ropes*)" (*ibid.*). In the current material both of these changes are seen in what can be described as hybrid types in the basic supplication form of core I:

(330) *rabbina yirḥamu* 'May our Lord have mercy on him'.

In (330) the subject *rabbina* 'our Lord' may be changed to *aḷḷāh* 'God', it may be omitted altogether or replaced by a different (and sometimes grammatically unjustified) form *ya rabb* 'oh, Lord'. The verb is usually imperfect, but imperative and perfective forms are also possible. This entails consequent changes to the form of the sentence. When the verb is changed to imperative, the subject might be *aḷḷāhumma* 'oh, God' or *ya rabb* 'oh, Lord' only. If the verb is perfective, the word order changes from SVO to VSO and also in terms of phonetic realisation, it will most probably be "elevated" to the standard variant. In the function of object usually 3rd person pronouns are used (*-u, -ha, -hum*), in their dialectal form. Sometimes (as in the case described above, but not only) the pronunciation might be standard, especially when dual forms appear (*humā*). All of them might, however, be changed into 2nd person pronouns in all of its forms. This operation is obviously not allowed with the imperative verb. Also, instead of pronouns, definite nouns referring to the deceased are possible in this place. However, this open class is limited semantically to people, including names, kinship terms (usually defined by a possessive pronoun), professional titles or

terms of endearment. This formula is sometimes intensified by selecting from a limited repertory of terms:
(331) *raḥma wasʿa* 'Great mercy'.
(332) *bi raḥmatihi/bi raḥmitu* 'With his mercy'.
(333) *bi raḥmitu l-wasʿa* 'With his great mercy'.
(334) *bi raḥmitak il-wasʿa* 'With your great mercy'.

Also, other forms are allowed as an expansion of this formula as in the following examples. These are not unlimited either, they must be related to living or dead people, usually close to the speaker in a way, e.g., as their family or community they belong to:
(335) *rabbina yirḥamu wi yirḥam bāba* 'May our Lord have mercy on him and my dad'.
(336) *rabbina yirḥamu huwwa wi abūya* 'May our Lord have mercy on him and my father'.
(337) *rabbina yirḥamha wi yirḥam mawtāna kulluhum* 'May our Lord have mercy on her and all deceased Muslims'.

What was said above applies equally to another formula possible in core I (338), where *rabbina* 'our Lord' can be changed to *aḷḷāh* 'God'. The verb can be made imperative or perfective, which entails changes in the subject and/or word order. The object pronoun can be changed from 3rd person to a 2nd person pronoun or to a noun referring to someone from the family (or another animate noun):
(338) *rabbina yiġfirlu* 'May our Lord have mercy on him'.

A structurally different formula (339) appearing in core I also belongs to this group. Here we have the word *raḥma* 'mercy', which is given attributives either before or after it (never before and after). Only a numeral *alf* 'thousand' may acceptably precede it. After the noun there are two possible options *aḷḷāh* 'God' and *rabbina* 'our Lord'. Their usage necessitates a change in the form of the noun *raḥma* > *raḥmit,* required in the genitive construction (*iḍāfa*). The predicate is always *ʿala* 'on' + 3rd or 2nd person pronoun. However, with (341) it does not have to appear, whereas with (339) and (340) it is obligatory. Finally, *alf raḥma* '[a thousand] mercy' is very often expanded to *alf raḥma wi nūr* '[a thousand] mercy and light', which elaborates the formula:
(339) *raḥmit aḷḷāh ʿalēh* 'God's mercy on him'.
(340) *raḥmit rabbina ʿalēh* 'Our Lord's mercy on him'.
(341) *alf raḥma* '[A thousand] mercy'.

One example in the material appeared modified in terms of word order:
(342) *ʿalēh raḥmit aḷḷāh* 'On him God's mercy'.

The formulae *rabbina yirḥamu* 'may our Lord have mercy on him' and *rabbina yiġfirlu* 'may our Lord forgive him' along with their possible variants appear in core II as well, however, in this location, the subject is omitted and the formula starts with *wa/wi* 'and'. Apart from that, all possible variants appearing in core I are also theoretically possible in core II. Furthermore, a number of alternative formulae based on different verbs appear (all of them in the imperfect tense): *yuḥsin* 'bestow good upon', *yaʿfū* 'forgive', *yisāmiḥ* 'forgive', *yatakarram* 'give generously', *yatagāwaz* 'forgive one's sins'. Probably because these verbs are rarer in this slot, their variability is limited. Also, the verbs in core II might have another complement referring to the notion of "sin":

(343) *yiġfirlu zunūbu* 'Forgive him his sins'.

(344) *yatagāwaz ʿan sayʾātu* 'May [he] forgive his sins'.

The same kind of variability is observable in supplement I. The most common example usually contains an imperfect verb, although imperative and perfect verbs are also possible:

(345) *wi yiskinu fasīḥ gannitu* 'And make him live in his vastest paradise'.

It might on certain occasions take an explicit subject in the form of *rabbina* 'our Lord' or the vocative *aḷḷāhumma* 'oh, God' (in which case the verb must be imperative). However, it is usually coordinated with *wi* 'and' with the preceding element. The object in most cases is the 3rd person pronoun, although the 2nd person pronoun appears there from time to time for stylistic reason or because the deceased was dear to the speaker. The second object always refers to heaven, although the nouns and NPs used to name it might vary considerably. The phrases are usually built around the nouns *al-ganna* 'garden' and *al-firdaws* 'heaven', but other verbalisations of the notion of heaven are also possible:

(346) *fasīḥ gannitu/gannitak/il-ginān* 'His/your/the vastest paradise'.

(347) *il-fardūs* [+ *il-aʾla* (+ *min il-ganna*)] 'The greatest garden of paradise'.

(348) *gannit il-fardūs il-ʾala* 'The garden of paradise'.

The formula usually ends here but might also be further expanded in a number of ways, e.g., referring to the afterlife as free from pain and penance (349), to the noble company one wishes the deceased to have in heaven (350) to God's mercy as a reason why the deceased should be blessed (351):

(349) *min ġēr ḥisāb wa lā sābiqa ʿaḏāb* 'Without being taken to account or torment'.

(350) *maʿa n-nabiyyīn wa ṣ-ṣadīqīn wa š-šuhadāʾ wa ṣ-ṣāliḥīn wa ḥusn ulāika rafīqan* 'With the prophets, the steadfast affirmers of truth, the martyrs and the righteous, and excellent are those as companions'.

(351) *bi raḥmitak* 'With your mercy'.

All of the added phrases use recursive religious forms.

Formulae with *yigʿal* 'make' present a great variety of supplications that fill the slot of supplement I. The verb appears mostly in the 3rd person singular of the imperfect tense, although sometimes the imperative occurs. The first of these formulae in its most common form is presented in (352), but other possible variants are illustrated in (353):

(352) *yigʿal maswāh il-ganna* 'May [God] make his abode heaven'.

(353) *yigʿal/igʿal* 'make' *maswa* 'abode'/*maʾwa* 'refuge' + 3rd/2nd *il-ganna* 'heaven' *(wa naʿimha* 'and its bliss'*)/il-fardūs il-aʿla* 'the greatest paradise'.

The formula *bidūn/min ġēr ḥisāb wa lā sābiqa ʿaḏāb* 'without being taken to account or torment' might be added in order to make it more elaborate. Another formula is presented below in its most common form (354) and its alternative variants (355):

(354) *yigʿal ʾabru rawḍa min riyāḍ il-ganna* 'May [God] make his grave a garden from the gardens of paradise'.

(355) *rabbina/aḻḻāhumma yigʿal/igʿal ʾabr* + 3rd *rawḍa min riyāḍ il-ganna* 'our Lord/oh God [may he] make his grave a garden from the gardens of paradise'.

Yet another formula featuring the verb *yigʿal* 'make' is presented in (356) and (357) along with its variants:

(356) *yigʿalu min ahl il-ganna* 'May [God] make him one of the dwellers of heaven'.

(357) *rabbina yigʿal/igʿal* 'May our Lord make' + 3rd/2nd *min ahl il-ganna* (*wi naʿimha*) 'one of the dwellers of heaven (and its bliss)'/*al-fardūs il-aʿla* (*min il-ganna*) 'the greatest paradise/garden (of heaven)'.

The last of the common formulae containing the verb *yigʿal* 'make' present the same variation as most of the formulae here. The last element is selected from a limited range of open class elements and is a PP starting with the preposition *fi* 'in'. The NP appearing after it is a name for heaven and presents a great variety of religious expressions, e.g.:

(358) *rabbina yigʿalu fi manzil aš-šuhadāʾ wa ṣ-ṣadīqīn* 'May Lord make him be in the house of martyrs and friends'.

(359) *yigʿalha fi l-fardūs il-aʿla min ġēr ḥisāb wa lā ʿaḏāb* 'May [God] make her [be] in the highest garden without being taken to account or torment'.

(360) *yigʿalu fi aʿla d-daraǧāt* 'May [God] make him [be] in the highest level'.

The phrase *min ġēr ḥisāb wa lā ʿaḏāb* 'without being taken to account or torment' appears additionally. This extension is also formulaic and might be added to any formula referring to the deceased being transferred to heaven.

A similar variation is seen in examples with *yudḫil* 'let in' (as well as *adḫal* and *adḫil)* and *yurzuʾ* 'grant' (also *urzuʾ*). Again, with *yudḫil* 'let in' in one example

rabbina 'our Lord' serves as a subject and with *urzu'* 'grant' the vocative *aḷḷāhum-ma* 'oh, God' appears three times. The objects are 3rd and 2nd person pronouns referring to the deceased and NPs referring to heaven. In the case of the latter, almost the same limited spectrum of NPs observed in previous formulae is used. Here with *yurzu'* 'grant' we have the somewhat intensified form:
(361) *yurzu'ha fū' in-naʿīm naʿīm* 'May [God] grant her bliss beyond all blisses'.

Also, as before, the phrase *bidūn ḥisāb wa lā sābiqa ʿaḏāb* 'without being taken to account or torment' or the shorter *bidūn ḥisāb* 'without being taken to account' is added to the formula. There are three examples of *bi izni ḷḷāh* 'with God's permission' added at the end as well.

The least adaptable seems to be the following short formula, where the variability involves the use or non-use of *rabbina* 'our Lord' as well as a change in the gender and number marking of the possessive pronouns attached to *'abr* 'grave':
(362) *rabbina yinawwar 'abru* 'May our Lord illuminate his grave'.

On the other hand, the greatest variability is observed in:
(363) *rabbina yigmaʿna bīhum fi l-ganna in šā' aḷḷāh* 'May our Lord unite us with them in heaven, God willing'.

Although in the material studied, the verb always is imperfective, a number of choices are possible with object pronouns: first person plural pronouns with an inclusive meaning "we" = "me and you", as well as second and third person singular and plural pronouns. With him/her/them might be replaced by with + kinship term (referring to the deceased). The terms for heaven cover a wider spectrum than in the previous cases, and more sophisticated formulae are used:
(364) *fi gannit il-ma'wa* 'In the garden of refuge'.
(365) *fī ǧannāt wa nahr wa maqʿad ṣidq mālik muqtadir* 'In the midst of gardens and rivers in an assembly of truth, in the presence of a sovereign omnipotent'.
(366) *fi mustaqirr raḥmitu* 'In the abiding abode of his mercy'[32].

Here, also *in šā' aḷḷāh* 'God willing' and *bi izni llāh* 'with God's permission' are possible as additional formulae. Sometimes *ʿala ḫēr* 'well' is added, which is also formulaic and appears in many blessings referring to future events.

Furthermore, supplement II provides examples of formulae with a limited range of variability in both function and content words. The expected
(367) *wi yisabbarak* 'And give you patience'

32 Translation: https://sunnah.com/adab:768, access: April 2021.

is often modified by adding *rabbina* 'our Lord' or *aḷḷāh* 'God' as the explicit subject. The second person pronoun is replaced with *ahl* 'family'+ 2nd or 3rd person possessive pronoun or with *'alb* 'heart' + 2nd person possessive pronoun. Kinship terms and terms of endearment also appear in this position. If the speaker is a relative or close friend of the deceased, the 1st person plural or even singular can be used. Most of the times the formula ends here; nevertheless, it can be completed with one of the following PPs introduced by *'ala* 'on':

(368) *'ala furā'* + 3rd person pronoun 'After the loss of'.

(369) *'ala l-furā'* 'After the loss'.

The last examples are the most common; however, other variants might appear rarely:

(370) *'alā l-ayyām al-qalīla bidūnikum* 'During these few days without you [plural]'.

(371) *'ala maṣābik* 'After the tragedy'.

With *yulhim ahlu ṣ-ṣabr* 'inspire his family with patience' the situation is similar. The subject *rabbina* 'our Lord' can be added to a verb. *Ahlu* 'his family', apart from the variation in possessive pronouns can also be expanded to *ahlu wi zawīh* 'his family and relatives'. The expression *wi s-silwān* 'and consolation' can be added *to aṣ-ṣabr* 'patience':

(372) *rabbina yulhim ahluhum wi zawīhum iṣ-ṣabr wi s-silwān* 'May Lord inspire their family and relatives with patience and consolation'.

Three other formulae follow the same pattern of variability in supplement II. Two of them show grammatical variability in the form of the verb: *yurzu'* 'grant', *yarbiṭ* 'make strong'. Two of the verbs are followed by 2nd person *(yurzu')* or 2nd/3rd person pronouns *(yi'awwi* 'strengthen'*)*. The PP following *'ala qalb/'ala qulūb* 'on + heart/hearts' is also accompanied by second/third person possessive pronouns. The noun *aṣ-ṣabr* in (373) might be additionally completed with *'ala l-furā'* 'after the loss'. The variation *'ala l-furā'/'ala furā'* + 3rd person possessive pronoun is also possible in (403):

(373) *yurzu'ak iṣ-ṣabr* 'May [God] give you patience'.

(374) *yi'awwīk 'ala furā'u* 'May [God] make you strong after your loss'.

(375) *yarbiṭ 'ala 'albik* 'May [God] give strength to your heart'.

In Wray's account even greater variability is visible in formulae that "have slots for open class items (e.g., *know SOMETHING like the back of ONE'S hand; give SOMEONE a piece of ONE'S mind*). Open class items are most often referential noun phrases, with pronouns particularly common" (2002: 50). In the material here, this type is exemplified mostly in formulae concerning the special case described in the previous chapter. Curses may take the following form (376), in which the presence of the explicit subject is optional:

(376) *rabbina yinti'im minnu* 'May Lord take revenge on him'.

Apart from this, in this particular case the 3rd person pronoun object might be changed to almost any noun or NP. Within this diversity, however, a certain repeating pattern emerges, consisting in the generalisations with the pronoun *kull* 'all':

(377) *rabbina yinti'im min kulli ẓālim* 'May our Lord take revenge on every oppressor'.

(378) *rabbina yinti'im min kull man kān lu īd fi ḥuznaha wi alamha* 'May our Lord take revenge on everyone who contributed to her sadness and pain'.

(379) *rabbina yinti'im min kull man yamnaʿ ḥu'ū' in-nās* 'May our Lord take revenge on everyone who violates other people's rights'.

What is more, the formula might be expanded in a way that may explain the manner in which the divine vengeance is to occur:

(380) *ašadd intiqām* 'The most severe revenge'.

(381) *aglan aw ʿāgilan* 'Sooner or later'.

The following formula allows for a very limited variability and appears in two forms:

(382) *ḥasbi ḷḷāh wa niʿma l-wakīl* 'God is sufficient for me and he is the best disposer of affairs'.

(383) *ḥasbina ḷḷāh wa miʿma l-wakīl* 'God is sufficient for me and he is the best disposer of affairs'.

However, it might be conventionally expanded with the preposition *fi* after which a noun or a NP might appears depending on the context. It this case too, a generalisation pattern with *kull* 'every' is present:

(384) *ḥasbi ḷḷāh wa niʿma l-wakīl fi man ẓalamha wi ḥaramha min il-awlād* 'God is sufficient for me and he is the best disposer of affairs against those who oppressed her and deprived her of the children'.

(385) *ḥasbi ḷḷāh wa niʿma l-wakīl fi kull man tasabbab fī qahriha* 'God is sufficient for me and he is the best disposer of affairs against those who made her suffer'.

(386) *ḥasbina ḷḷāh wa niʿma l-wakīl fi kull ab yiḥrim umm min awladha* 'God is sufficient for me and he is the best disposer of affairs against every father depriving a mother of her children'.

The same is observed in the formula starting with:

(387) *(rabbina) yiʿawwiḍ* 'May our Lord compensate' + 2nd/3rd person pronoun.

This blessing might be completed with expressions such as: *ḫēr* 'well' or *bi l-ganna* 'in heaven', or with a PP starting with *ʿan* 'for' and containing any kind of information referring to the idea of the harm that requires compensation:

(388) *rabbina yiʿawwiḍha ḫēr* 'May our Lord compensate her well'.

(389) *rabbina yiʿawwiḍha ʿan kull alam šafithu fi d-dinya* 'May our Lord compensate her for what she experienced [saw] in her life'.

The fragments of prayers represent a profound level of formulaicity, although when used in response to death announcements, they may not be part of the conventional repertoire of forms. They represent right-hemispheric language – texts remembered in connection with the situation of death, inextricably linked with the context of their occurrence and specific emotions associated with the phonetic form, recalled automatically. In their case, variability tends to occur as a freedom when ordering the recalled elements; therefore, the phrases from the prayers are combined arbitrarily to some extent (still, the lines of prayers are often cited in their correct order). This combination generally meets the requirements of logic and pragmatics:
(390) *aḷḷāhumma abdilhā dāran ḫayran min dārihā wa ahlan ḫayran min ahlihā* 'Oh, God, give her home better than her home and family better than her family'.
(391) *wa mā ṣabrak illā min ʿind aḷḷāh* 'And your patience is not but through God'.

To summarise the account on variability in formulae referring to the taboo of death, three levels might be distinguished:

- fixed formulae,
- formulae with limited grammatical and lexical variability,
- formulae with slots for open class items.

To this a few words may be added about the often-described phenomenon of omission. As for the subject, it usually appears in the first part of the core only – supplication for mercy for the deceased. The next elements are introduced with the conjunction *wi* or *wa* 'and'. This does not constitute any deviation from the natural mode of expression. Sometimes, however, even in core I, the examples abbreviated formulae that contain no explicit subject are provided. There are also situations (and these are relatively common) when the invocation *ya rabb* 'our Lord' is used before the formula and, in such case, the omission of the subject sounds natural:
(392) *ya rabb yirḥamu wi yiġfirlu wi yigʿalu fi l-fardūs il-aʿla* 'Oh, Lord, [may he] have mercy on him and forgive him, and make him live in the greatest paradise'.

Omitting verbs is not very common either. Ferguson, regarding the Syrian formulae, says that "[t]he only God-wish in which the verb is usually omitted is *aḷḷāh* (*yikūn*) *maʿāk* 'God [be] with you' in which the copula is optional" (Ferguson 1997a: 225). In the current material an equivalent expression occurs once in supplement II:
(394) *rabbina maʿāk* 'May our Lord be with you'.

Also, a specific type of formulae appearing in supplement I usually lack a verb (393)–(394), although it might also be used (395):
(393) *fi l-ganna wi naʿimha in šāʾ aḷḷāh* 'In heaven and its bliss, God willing'.
(394) *fi l-ganna bi izni llāh* 'In heaven, with God's permission'.
(395) *yinʿam fi gannit aḷḷāh bi izni llāh* 'May he bask in the garden of God, with God's permission'.

Occasionally the object might be omitted, however, these examples are extremely rare in the material, and have additional stylistic value:
(396) *ya rabb hawwin, ya rabb hawwin, ya rabb hawwin* 'Oh, Lord, make it easier, oh, Lord, make it easier, oh, Lord, make it easier'.
(397) *ya rabb iġfir wi irḥam wi akrim* 'Oh, Lord, forgive and have mercy, and give generously'.

Wray (2002) also mentions that for some idioms, certain modifications to the grammatical structure, e.g., passivisation, result in the loss of idiomaticity:
(398) *the bucket was kicked (AW).

This creates room for linguistic creativity, however, examples of it were not found in the current material except in the special case. This is probably because the vast majority of the people commenting on it did not belong to the family nor were close friends of the deceased. For them, the sense of tabooisation of the subject may have been relatively minor. It seems that the taboo blocks the linguistic creativity in a way. Examples include:
(399) *aw huwwa fiʿlan aḷḷāh raḥamha min il-qaswa wi l-alam wi l-qahr da* 'Or maybe God really relieved her from cruelty, pain and oppression?'.

Instead of the optative mood, the past tense was used in the example above, which is additionally emphasised by the use of *fiʿlan* (probably to make sure the intended non-formulaic meaning is conveyed). Therefore, this expression cannot be read as a blessing or supplication:
(400) *dilwaʾti rabbina hayigmaʿha bīhum fi l-ganna in šāʾ aḷḷāh* 'Now our Lord will unite her with them in heaven, God willing'.

In the next sentence the future tense is used with a conventional blessing structure which deactivates the formulaic aspect of the expression. Also, the word *dilwaʾti* 'now' signals analytical rather formulaic reading. However, *in šāʾ aḷḷāh* 'God willing' is used to mitigate the certainty of the statement.

A unique phenomenon in the studied material is the embedding of one formula within another, an example of which is the sentence below, where *in šāʾ aḷḷāh* appears as an insertion in the middle of the blessing:

(401) *yigmaʿna bīhum in šāʾ aḻḻāh fi l-ganna* 'May our Lord unite us with them, God willing, in heaven'.

In šāʾ aḻḻāh 'God willing' and *bi izni llāh* 'with God's permission' often appear at the end of formulae wishing the deceased a place in heaven, especially when these formulae appear without a verb (the formula is not in optative mood). When blessing comes in the form of assurance as in (402) these expressions are usually accompanied with *in šāʾ aḻḻāh,* which is often used as a method of hedging. One simply does not want to make impression of being able to predict God's actions. On the other hand, they are practically never met after any of the wishes in the core:
(402) *fi l-ganna in šāʾ aḻḻāh* 'In heaven, God willing'.
(403) *tkūn fi makān agmal wi aḥla wi aḥsan min hina* 'May she be in a place that is more beautiful, prettier and better than here'.

At first glance, these formulae would seem to testify to a fatalistic outlook on life in the Muslim society. However, as Feghali notices *in šāʾ aḻḻāh*

> is very frequently used by Arabic speakers and, according to Condon and Yousef (1975) reflects a present-orientedness in society. While claims have been forwarded that such a worldview is fatalistic and has negative consequences for business and national development, others state more mundane roots of these problems (Palmer, Leila, & Yassin, 1988). Nydell (1987) specifies that the "belief that God has direct and ultimate control of all that happens" (p. 34) has been overemphasized by Westerners and is far more prevalent among traditional, uneducated people in the region (1997: 367).

The author refers to the universality of this formula in the everyday life of Muslims and its ambiguity:

> *Inshallah* used in a variety of ways to regulate social interaction by alluding to the possibilities that an action may or may not take place. More specifically, *inshallah* may mean: "yes" at some unspecified future time; "no", in terms of "a refusal to make a serious commitment, to take personal responsibility, or even attempt to deflect the blame for failure for promised action to take place" (...). Attending to the placement of *inshallah* in a sentence, the presence of the medial glottal stop, and the intonation with which it is spoken may reveal which response is being communicated (Stevens, 1991). This delineation of alternative meanings reflects active attempts to coordinate and control interaction (*ibid.*).

Regarding the current study, it seems that *in šāʾ aḻḻāh* as well as *bi izni llāh* prevent the interpretation that the speaker is excessively audacious about future actions taken by God.

7.5. Intensifying formulae

One of the main characteristics of the ways of consoling people in Egyptian culture is to convey God's blessing on them, in which several different polite strategies may be performed at once. Such a usage aims to soothe and comfort those mourning the death of the loved ones through the embellishment of death, distancing, optimism, asserting common ground by including themselves in the suffering. Some of the utterances encountered in the current material have an exuberant character and the expressions are often combined to strengthen the effect. The Maxim of Quantity (Grice 1975) is flouted, repetition of the same meaning in different grammatical and lexical structures is employed. Furthermore, a strategy based on the "lots of form = lots of content" scheme is adopted; the elaboration, repetition and the use of intensifiers maximises the consolation, with almost cathartic powers.

A salient feature of the Egyptian Arabic way of conveying consolation is through intense and effusive displays of affection. A number of techniques are used to maximise the message. When consoling a close friend usually more than one formula is used at a time. Nonconventional forms also have the function of intensifying the message. The speaker tries to communicate the sincerity of his/her intentions to the recipient by deviating from the accepted standard forms and opting for a more personalised expression or, contrarily, choosing a sophisticated one:

(404) *yunzil bard as-sakīna wa r-riḍā' ʿala qulūb kull aḥibbā'ihi* 'May [God] send the cold of peace and acceptance on the hearts of all his loved ones'.

(405) *yigmaʿkum ʿala ḫēr ʿandu fi d-daragāt il-ʿula min il-ganna bi guwār sayyidna muḥammad il-muḫtār ṣalla aḻḻāh ʿalēh* 'May [God] unite you [well] in his home in the greatest level of heaven in the neighbourhood of Muhammad, the chosen one, peace be upon him'.

(406) *yi'nisu fi waḥšit 'abru wi yimidd baṣaru wi yigʿalu rawḍa min riyāḍ il-ganna wi yurzu'u naʿimha* 'And may [God] accompany him in the loneliness of the grave and extend his eyesight, and make his grave a garden from the gardens of paradise'.

Some elements of supplications might be intensified lexically:

(407) *yurzu'ha fū' in-naʿīm naʿīm* 'Bestow upon her bliss that is beyond all blisses'.

Terms of address are also used to enforce the message; they might include terms of endearment, e.g., *ḥabībi* 'my love'/'my dear' or, more often, the addressee's name. Sometimes, they are addressed directly at the deceased person. They were here classified as DMs, because they always appear peripherally before or after formulae.

One of the methods of intensification is *al-mafʿūl al-muṭlaq*, a relatively rare, paronomastic echoing of the root. It also introduces an extra nuance to the meaning in the form of an attributive added to the *maṣdar* (verbal noun), as in the following example:

(408) *rabbina yiṣabbarik ʿala furāʾu ṣabran gamīlan* 'May Lord give you [beautiful] patience after the loss'.

Repetitions are one of the main features of the EA style, both in speech and in the written form. They serve the function of intensifying the message, strengthening the effect and giving the utterance an exuberant character. They appear in many different grammatical and lexical structures, for instance as the root repetition:

(409) *aḷḷāhumma farriǧ humūm al-mahmūmīn* 'Oh, God, drive away the troubles of the troubled'.

Usually, the psychological scheme of "more form = more content" is operative at the moment of their production. Repetitions are used when the utterance is felt not to be expressive enough. In response to condolences direct repetitions occur as well:

(410) *amīn amīn amīn ya rabb il-ʿalamīn* 'Amen, amen, amen, oh, Lord of the worlds'.

Additionally, an important feature of the Egyptian etiquette system is adjuration; it plays a role of intensifying the positive politeness, reinforcing and confirming speaker's intentions and expressing his/her sincerity. Adjuration appears in most online conversations; whenever there is an interaction between two friends, a field for adjuration opens. The most frequent examples are: *waḷḷāhi* 'by God' or *waḷḷāhi l-ʿaẓīm* 'by God, the greatest', *wa n-nabi* 'by the Prophet', *wa ḥyat rabbina* 'by the life of our Lord', *wa ḥyātak* 'by your life'. *Bi gadd* 'seriously' plays a very similar function to the most conventionalised examples of adjuration, therefore, it may be classified as having the same pragmatic function. An interesting founding in both the 2016 study and the current work is that adjuration in its function of reinforcing the message and strengthening positive politeness is usually found in examples where the sincerity of speaker's intentions might be subject to doubt. On the other hand, in such cases as condolences, where sincerity is out of question, adjuration usually does not occur.

Although a common feature of CMC is the use of emoticons and graphic equivalents of non-verbal aspects of speech normally present in face-to-face communication for intensifying the emotional load of the utterance, however, they are barely present in the analysed material. This is probably due to the seriousness of the topic. In death announcements and replies to them, the only examples of this kind appeared in DM slots and always concerned the invocation *ya rabb* (e.g. the aliph [ā] was repeated several times to denote the extension of the vowel):

(411) *yaaaa rabb il-ʿalamīn* (ياااارب العالمين) 'Oh, Lord of the worlds'.

7.6. Grammaticalisation

Grammaticalisation defined as the "attribution of a grammatical character to a formerly autonomous word" (Meillet 1912) is seen whenever there is a decrease in the amount of semantic information for a lexical item or other linguistic unit. It is also thought to be one of the greatest motors of change in language. With grammaticalisation changes proceed from concrete to abstract. The reason why this issue may concern formulae related to death is their conventionality leading at times to reduction of form and referential meaning of the phrases. The formulae might be syntactically idiosyncratic and also violate other linguistic rules. This may be a reason why one should think about the formulae used in reaction to the taboo of death as ritual behaviour. They contain at least the first of 4 steps of grammaticalisation distinguished by Heine: 1) desemantisation (semantic bleaching); 2) extension (extending the form to new contexts); 3) decategorialisation (reduction or loss of morphosyntactic properties); 4) erosion (phonetic reduction) (2003: 579). "Semantic impoverishment is one of the most broadly discussed issues in assessing the level of grammaticalization (Heine 2003; Heine and Reh 1984; Hopper 1996) and the common belief is that a high level of grammaticalization involves losing the complexity and richness of the semantic content, especially when intensifiers are considered" (Zawrotna 2018). The conclusion, then, would be that perhaps the formulae discussed here are evolutionarily at some stage of grammaticalisation.

Looking more broadly at the subject of death, it is possible to recognise certain patterns of desemantisation in the Egyptian dialect. In EA the word "death" is a source of intensifiers because it is taboo:

(412) *waḥišni mōt* 'I miss you to death [like death]' (MZ).
(413) *baḥibbik mōt* 'I love you to death [like death]' (MZ).
(414) *bamūt fīki* 'I adore you' ['I am dying about you'] (MZ).

The examples above show that both the noun "death" and verb "to die" serve as intensifiers and are used in an overtly positive type of context. The development of *mōt* 'death' into an intensifier included a change of category from noun to intensifying adverbial. This word can also be used without an article after a definite noun phrase (Woidich 2018):

(415) *il-banāt il-ḥilwa mōt* 'The terribly nice girls' (MW).

The noun 'death' and verb 'to die' can both be used as intensifiers in a variety of contexts and have lost, in these cases, their primary semantic value. The source of their intensifying power is based on the extremity of death in human experience.

In order to serve as an intensifier, a word must undergo a process of grammaticalisation associated with the loss of its referential meaning. An extremely interesting process takes place here, in which taboo becomes the motor of grammaticalisation, but at the same time, the taboo character is lost in the same process. The word 'death' as an intensifier is neutral in terms of tabooisation. This is another way in which the word functions linguistically (death was previously mentioned as a situational taboo – when it concerns the interlocutors directly, and as a neutral word). In this material, death is strongly tabooed and largely displaced from use. The word *mawt* 'death' does not appear once, instead a euphemism *wafāt* 'death' appears in a few death announcements. The verb *māt* 'to die' is rare as well and occurs 6 times. None of these words are encountered in comments and dialogues.

7.7. Problems with language

While using CMC data, a few problems emerge in terms of language in Egypt resulting mainly from diglossia. The existence of a continuum of language varieties is increasingly complicated in relation to formulae by the fact that they sometimes reflect past stages of language. The formulae often originate in the Quran or the Hadith and so their form is classical. The mere statement that the formulae present fossilised forms in language would not yet be a complete description, because there are significant differences among them regarding their fixedness. The blessings used at present employ the imperfective optative, but nevertheless their use is arbitrary to some extent. Blessings with a verb in perfect tense also appear, which is a marked choice and bears the features of linguistic stylisation by rendering the expression more solemn. This dependence is linked to word order – in modernised (dialectal) formulae the SVO order pertains with the imperfective verb, while the VSO order is associated with classical form and used with a perfective verb.

This, however, does not provide the actual picture. It turns out that the formulae can be phonetically implemented in many ways. Sometimes they adopt dialectal phonetics, especially when elements of novel language appear alongside them with personal comments. The group *raḥamahu* might be as well pronounced as *raḥamu.* Still, sometimes the same formulae are pronounced according to CA phonology, which may be determined by the proximity of rare formulae, e.g., memorised during prayers in a mosque or by recitation of the Quran. The environment of the utterance may also prove decisive – if a death announcement is accompanied by many comments from different people, we often notice a unification of the style and similar formulae being used. Some utterances influence others. The manner of pronunciation is strongly contextualised, a clear example of which is the fact that the native speaker, who was asked to read aloud all the formulae contained in the material analysed here, often read them in two different ways, unable to decide

on one pronunciation without context. When deciding on the dialectal variant, he commented several times that during prayers in a mosque or in the house of the deceased, a given formula should be pronounced differently. Some forms are automatically pronounced dialectally:
(416) *rabbina yisabbarkum* 'May our Lord give you patience'.

Others contain "hints" as to the intentions of the writer, e.g., a long [ī] indicates dialectal pronunciation in *bīhum* 'with them':
(417) *yigmaʿik bīhum fi l-ganna* 'May [God] unite you with them in heaven'.

In other cases, the spelling might suggest a standard pronunciation, such as in forms with the dual pronoun:
(418) *aḷḷāh yarḥamuhumā* 'May God have mercy on them (dual)'.

Also, the opposition of *rabbina*/*aḷḷāh* as a subject might suggest how it should be read. *Rabbina* is a more local version (in Egypt the form *rabbi* 'my Lord' is practically out of use), and *aḷḷāh* occurs more often (but not always) in classical expressions. Additionally, the level of precision in standard pronunciation varies, which may also affect the perception of the degree of solemnity of these forms. The above considerations lead to the conclusion that formulae in Egyptian Arabic are subject to another type of variability in the morphophonetic dimension, closely related to pragmatic and stylistic conditions. The illocutionary power of dialectal expressions is different from that of the classical ones, and so is their effect. This is in line with Wray's findings on oral traditions that bind the use of formulaic sequences "with the particular demands of the genre or activity of which they form a part" (2002: 75).

7.8. Curses

Apart from the blessings, the material also includes a significant number of curses relating to the special case:
(419) *rabbina yintiʾim min kull man kān lu īd fi ḥuznaha wi alamha u rabbina huwa l-muntaʾim il-gabbār* 'May our Lord take revenge on everyone who contributed to her sadness and pain, our Lord is a mighty avenger'.
(420) *aḷḷāhumma ntiʾim min kulli ẓālim ṭāġi* 'Oh, God, take revenge on every unjust oppressor'.
(421) *rabbina yiḥrimu min ir-rāḥa wi min ir-raḥma wi yidūʾ ṭaʿm il-garīma lli ʿamalha la ḥadd ma yudḫul il-ʾabr* 'May Lord deprive him of comfort and mercy, may he be tasting the crime he committed until he enters the tomb'.

(422) *rabbina yizillu fi d-dunya wa l-āḫira* 'May God condemn him in this world and in the afterlife'.

D'Anna defines a curse as "a wish expressed verbally for something bad to befall a certain person or object (...). Curses may or may not take the form of a prayer" (2014: 49). Hamady (1960: 169) believes a curse intends injury. The evil wish is realised by "the mysterious power of the curse itself or by the aid of a supernatural being invoked in it" (*ibid.*). It can thus be either fully magical or it can be similar to a prayer. Hamady also makes a distinction between categorical and conditional curses. Categorical ones become operative at the moment of their pronouncement, while in the case of conditional curses (oaths) the evil happens to the speaker him-/herself, should their words not be true (*ibid.*). Usually curses have a very similar structure to blessings or *duʿā*. There is a religious prohibition on swearing in the minds of Egyptians, expressed more explicitly in the Hadith (Masliyah 2001: 268). At the same time, in the Quran we find examples of cursing nonbelievers, but, curiously enough, there is also a ban on cursing their idols (Masliyah 2001: 108). Arabic verb *laʿan* 'curse' is often pronounced metathetically as *naʿal* for taboo reasons. It is used in curses the same way the word *bārak* 'bless' is used in blessings.

D'Anna mentions such techniques as: (1) reference to obscenities and body parts or (2) targeting the opponent's family, as well as those apparently unacceptable in traditional Arab society, e.g., (3) targeting religion. Cursing religion is a heavily stigmatised form of linguistic behaviour in Egypt. In Muslim society, tradition forbids the insult of religion and such an offence is classified as one of the most serious sins (called in Arabic *sabb ad-dīn*). At the same time, despite the social stigmatisation, such curses are found among the basic techniques of forming insults. Among other examples of swearing, lexical forms using the optative perfect tense (currently considered archaic) should be mentioned (Woidich 1995: 261):
(423) *ḫadak rabbina* 'May our Lord take you!' (DS).
(424) *miskak ʿafrīt* 'May a demon grab you!' (DS).

Most of them are considered fixed expressions. From a formal point of view, the most frequently met are curses based on *aḷḷāh yilʿan/yinʿal* 'may God curse' or the elliptical *yilʿan/yinʿal* and *gak/gatak* 'may *x* befall'. Today the structure that uses the optative imperfect is more productive.
(425) *yiḫrib bētak* 'May God destroy your house'.
(426) *yilʿan abu šaklak* 'May your appearance be cursed'.
(427) *yilʿan mayyitīn ummak* 'May your mother's ancestors be cursed'.

Curses probably originate from spells – performative speech acts based on the belief in the causal power of words. This understanding is confirmed in the

Egyptian dialect by the presence of a separate grammatical category, which appears in blessings and curses, namely the root-echo response. Such responses are based on paronomasia which, according to D'Anna, highlights the "magical powers" of language (2014: 277). This category was thoroughly described by Stewart (1997).

Curses often, but not necessarily, refer to supernatural agency, with God as an agent. They are, roughly speaking, requests addressed to God for some evil to befall an opponent. The conversations I have conducted with Egyptians suggest that the curse (*la'na*) is understood literally as requesting God to send a disaster such as illness or wealth loss. In addition, numbers appearing in curses, often the multiplications of 60 (e.g. 60,000), seem to confirm the thesis regarding the magical origin of these expressions:

(428) *gatak sittīn nīla* 'Go to sixty hells'.

(429) *ġūri fi sittīn dahya* 'Go to sixty hells'.

According to Stewart, "The curses in general invoke some sort of higher or supernatural agency but only rarely mention God specifically. Others simply mention the immediate affliction or agent which will cause the hoped-for damage" (1997: 332). In fact, many curses have in their structure the name of God, but it is often elided for example: *aḷḷāh yiḫrib bētak* 'may God destroy your house' > *yiḫrib bētak* 'destroy your house', *aḷḷāh yiḥra' dīnak* 'may God burn your religion' > *yiḥra' dīnak* 'burn your religion'. Some of the curses, such as *ḫadak rabbina* 'may our Lord take you!' cannot occur without the operating agent mentioned. In the material studied referring to "the special case", most curses did mention God as an agent (for instance 28 out of 43 examples with the verb *yinti'im* 'to take revenge'). Examples without subject were also relatively numerous, both for structured curses and for other types of expressions similar to them in terms of meaning and function:

(430) *ḥayinti'im minnu agilan aw 'āgilan* '[God] will take revenge on him sooner or later'.

(431) *minnu li llāh yitṣarraf fīh* 'May he go to Hell [may God punish him], [may God] treat him [properly]'.

Example (431) starts with a colloquial expression followed by a request to God for intervention. Curses often take the form of praising God's qualities:

(432) *yumhil wa lā yuhmil, huwwa l-munta'im il-gabbār* 'God's mill grinds slow but sure, he is a mighty avenger'.

The example above and the following as well additionally remind of God's justice:

(433) *yu'ṭi kull wāḥid 'ala 'add 'amalu* '[God] will reward every man according to his deeds'.

Some expressions do not have the typical form of a curse, therefore, God does not act as an agent at all, and the following example expresses a wish:

(434) *li yiḥya huwa fi nār id-dunya bi mā ganāh* 'May he live in the hell of earthly life after what he did'.

On the other hand, examples occur having a classical or even archaising form:

(435) *la'nit aḷḷāh 'alēh wi 'ala 'araybu* 'May he and his family be cursed by God'.

(436) *ya waylu min rabbina huwa willi sa'du 'ala kida* 'Woe unto him and those who helped him'.

8. Recapitulation of the analysed material

In the previous chapters, the structure of the formulae used when speaking about death (announcing, acknowledging, reacting, and entering an interaction with a mourner) was presented. Some of their features, e.g., prefabricated language elements, were also discussed, including their variability. Formulaic language constitutes a relatively small percentage of death announcements, but it dominates the rest of the speech acts examined here. The death announcements researched, although only 20 randomly selected examples were analysed, follow many different models. Due to their diversity and the limited amount of material, no attempt was made to classify them, as any conclusions drawn this way would not be reliable. Analysing data obtained from sources other than CMC would probably produce different results. Al-Khatib and Salem (2011) studied Muslim and Christian obituaries in Jordanian Arabic newspapers. They discovered far more formalised structures in them. In their corpus, 65% of the obituaries were rounded off by a what is referred to here as a framing formula, appearing mostly in reactions to death announcements. In Christian obituaries representing 1% of their material, this formula was replaced with the Biblical verse: *ʔarrab ʔaʕtaa wa ʔarrab ʔaxð. fal yakun ismu ʔarrabi mubarakan* 'The Lord gave and the Lord has taken away. Blessed be the name of the Lord'. Invocations to God and prayers for a place in heaven for the deceased accounted for 30% of their material, though qualitatively these were different from those appearing in the Egyptian CMC. The authors summarised their analysis as follows: "most of Jordanian obituaries included verses from the Holy Quran and the Bible as well as many prayers for the deceased. The opening and closing parts of the obituaries were verses from either the Holy Quran or the Bible. Invoking God to forgive the deceased and let him/her enter paradise was a common feature of Jordanian obituaries" (2011: 93). Obituaries in the newspapers have a more formalised structure than personal posts on private social media profiles. In terms of structure, the texts appearing in them tended to correspond to the comments to the posts in the corpus analysed in the current study. These answers not only appear in abundance, but also use largely formulaic language, mostly following the scheme described in Structural Notes. Reacting to death is based on group rituals: linguistic items appear in their expected places. There is also a certain range of typical deviations from this norm, e.g., sometimes quotations from prayers occur and sometimes nonformulaic texts appear, although each time it seems to be justified somehow. Such examples are rarely found standing alone, but tend to accompany the expected formulaic response.

(opening formula > framing formula > core I > core II > supplement I > supplement II > framing formula > closing formula)

Figure 1. The structure of a typical comment

A typical scheme of combining formulae is presented at the beginning of the structural analysis. Accordingly, the comment made in response to death announcement begins with the opening formula related in general to divine omnipotence, followed by a framing formula that refers specifically to death. Next in line is the crucial core I formula, which takes the form of a supplication and requests mercy for the deceased. It usually begins with the subject (most often a *rabbina* 'Lord', sometimes *allah* 'God'), followed by an imperfect verb. The conjunction *wi* 'and' introduces core I, in which the speaker asks God for forgiveness for the deceased. The next element is a two-part supplement, in which each element is introduced by *wi*/*wa*. The first part refers to the deceased – here the speaker asks God for a place in heaven for him/her. The next part is a supplication addressed to God to provide the sufferer with patience after the loss. A framing formula or closing formula may appear at the end, unless they have already occurred. This scheme is rarely realised in its entirety; usually the speaker uses only a few selected formulae. The order presented here does not apply in 100% of the comments, however, in the material studied, there were only a few examples in which it was disturbed. The portions of material to which the model proposed here did not apply were of two types – non formulaic, non-religious comments appearing occasionally and, on the other hand – prayers, poetic and other non-classifiable forms of expression, which constitute a minority in the material:

(437) *lā ḥāwl wa lā quwwa illa bi ḷḷāh, al-baqā' li llāh, rabbina yirḥamu wi yiġfirlu wi yiskinu fasīḥ gannitu wi yisabbarak* 'There is no power and no strength save in God, only God is eternal, may our Lord have mercy on him and forgive him, and make him live in his vastest paradise, and give you patience'.

Between the opening and framing formulae, the conjunction *wa/wi* 'and' never appears. Likewise, core I usually begins as a separate entity and is not linked to the previous elements of the utterance by any conjunction. Regarding the connections between slots, it is important to mention the discourse markers occurring between these formulae (but never between the opening and framing formula).

In the schema distinguished here, some formulae are more obligatory than others, although none is compulsory. The most common is core I (73.4%) and this form itself can be used instead of a multi-formula whole. However, reactions lacking this part also appear; they usually fall into three groups: expressions that consist only of a framing formula (the second formula that can replace a multi-formula comment), nonformulaic expressions and prayers/poems. The first of these groups can be considered a conventional reaction, while the other two are rarer.

Core II appears in 43.9% of the examples and never occurs without core I. Supplement I and II are present respectively in 43% and 24.1% of the material, they are therefore optional elements. The rarest in the material are framing formulae and opening/closing formulae. Formulae normally associated with a different context of use are extremely rare, such as *aḷḷāhu akbar* 'God is the greatest' appearing three times in place of the opening formula:

(438) *aḷḷāhu akbar, aḷḷāh yirḥmha* 'God is the greatest, may God have mercy on her'.

Discourse markers appear in between formulae and terms of address and personal name are often used. A direct address to the deceased like: *ya ʿamm ḥasan* 'uncle Hasan', *ʿamm maḥmūd* 'uncle Mahmud' serves to underline the fact that the one who died was close to the speaker and express solidarity with his/her family.

The acceptance of condolences is often communicated by *amīn* 'amen', *aḷḷāhumma amīn* 'oh, God, amen' or *amīn ya rabb* 'amen, oh Lord'. The condoled person may express thanks by conveying blessing on the speaker: *gazākum aḷḷāh gamīʿan kull il-ḫayr wa gaʿal duʿākum fi mizānkum* 'may God reward all of you with his goodness, and consider your prayers on the day of judgment', *yiḫallīki liyya wi yibarikli fīki ya rabb* 'may [God] keep you safe for me and bless you, oh, Lord', *ǧazākum aḷḷāh dā'iman kull al-ḫayr wa mā 'arākum šarran fī man tuḥibbūna 'abadan* 'may God always reward you with the goodness and make you never see evil in who you love'. A "thank you" is almost never given in response. In the current study, mourners thanked only those who commented in English and these comments were not included in the corpus because their authors were not Egyptians.

Ferguson notices a somewhat similar phenomenon in his study of Syrian formulae: "In these responses the replier does not seem to be thanking the questioner, but rather thanking God for the state of his own health" (1997a: 223).

The formulae appearing in the material fulfil various pragmatic functions. Asking for prayers often replaces direct information about death or suffering:

(439) *tid'ilna kida* 'Pray for me'.

(440) *as'alukum ad-du'ā' li ḫāli* 'I ask you to pray for my uncle'.

It even happens that the formula of supplication for mercy is used to indirectly express criticism. The example below is one of the comments found in the "special case". Several commenters took the side of the ex-husband of the deceased woman. Their comments were intended to end the wave of curses that befell him. Typically, they did not contain any elements of blessing, although the example below includes the formula of core I accompanied by a request to stop the photos of the deceased from being published. In this context, the formula instead functions as a critique.

(441) *balāš iṣ-ṣiwar di law samaḥti rabbina yirḥamha* 'Enough of these pictures, please, may our Lord have mercy on her'.

Ferguson points out that using formulae containing blessings performs various pragmatic functions in Semitic languages: "The use of a formula of blessing as a salutation on certain occasions is a well-attested phenomenon in speech communities using Semitic languages (Plassmann 1913: 138–139; Lande 1949: 9–11), and it is especially well documented for Arabic-speaking communities in the Syria-Palestine area (cf. e.g., Barthelemy 1935–1954 s.v. *br k)"* (Ferguson 1997c). As mentioned earlier, in Egyptian Arabic the expression *aḷḷāh yiḥallīk* 'may God keep you safe' has the status of a conventional formula in the sense of "please". Ferguson writes: "The begging-and-thanking use of God-wishes referring to life-preservation is analogous in many respects to regular patterns of semantic extension, as when diminutives referring to size in Arabic or other languages are extended to indicate affection, and the same formal devices might be employed to describe it" (1997a: 227). In many cases found in the material God is called a name that expresses a feature of him sought at the moment, e.g. *al-munta'im* 'avenger', when revenge is needed:

(442) *huwwa arḥam ir-raḥimīn* 'He is the most merciful'.

(443) *rabbina il-munta'im il-gabbār* 'Our Lord is a mighty avenger'.

Death announcements appearing in the present material, to some extent, elude the scheme described in other works on the discourse of death, where one avoids mentioning death directly; instead, implicit reference is preferable. Here, on the other hand, a direct reference to death and dying is made in a few examples. Additionally, no repetitive pattern of announcing death occurs. The situation is different in the case of responses to them, which are highly schematic in nature, and the theme of death is treated in a manner mediated by religious experience. If we were to address the subject in the light of the theory of politeness (Brown and Levinson 1987), which directly relates to interpersonal interaction, we could conclude that a speaker conveying or reacting to an information about someone's death is in danger of committing a face-threatening act. Therefore, he/she chooses from among positive and negative politeness strategies – both seem to be used, with a preference for the "be conventionally indirect" negative strategy[33]. Although some Internet users are comfortable with expressions such as: *māt/mātit* 'died', most people prefer at least a minimum level of indirectness, as in the euphemism: *itwaffa* 'passed away'. Even more indirect are statements such as: *rāh is-sama* 'went do heaven'.

Another characteristic feature of the material studied is the multiplicity of formulae and repetitive expressing similar blessing and supplications. Feghali recognises two patterns of communication influencing the perception[34] of Arab rhetoric as "elaborate", these are exaggeration and assertion. The author also believes that both of them are used as tools for building the credibility of the speaker towards the audience (Feghali 1997). In line with the principle that more form means more content, exuberance is considered more cordial and is "recommended" while condoling a relative or a close friend:

(444) *lā ḥawl wa lā quwwa 'illā bi ḷḷāh, al-biqā' li ḷḷāh, ḥabībati, aḷḷāhumma yiṯabbituha 'ind as-su'āl wa ġfir lanā wa rzuqhā al-firdaws al-'a'lā, 'aẓẓam aḷḷāhu ağrakum* 'There is no power and no strength save in God, only God is eternal, my dear, oh, God, keep her strong when she is asked [by the angels] and forgive us [our sins] and grant her [life in] in his vastest paradise, God reward your patience'.

(445) *rabbina yirḥamu wi yiġfirlu wi yagma'kum bīh fi l-ganna ba'd 'umr ṭawīl fi ṭā'it rabbina in šā' aḷḷāh* 'May our Lord have mercy on him and let you meet with him/her in heaven after a long life in the service of our Lord, God willing'.

(446) *aḷḷāhumma ġfir lahu wa rḥamhu wa adẖilhu fasīḥ ğannatika yā 'arḥam ar-raḥīmīn wa iğ'alhu yā rabb min 'utaqā' šahr ramaḍān yā rabb* 'Oh, God, forgive his sins and have mercy on him and let him into your vastest heaven, the most merciful, and let him, oh Lord, among those who are freed in the month of Ramadan, oh Lord'.

In many examples another feature of Arabic style is visible, namely, repetition, as in:

33 A full account on positive and negative strategies of politeness can be found in Brown and Levinson (1987: 102, 131).

34 Górska (2015) notices the popular perception of Arabic as „intensive".

(447) *tkūn fi makān agmal wi aḥla wi aḥsan* 'May you be in a more beautiful [and prettier] and better place'.
(448) *amīn amīn amīn gazākum aḷḷāh gamīʿan kull il-ḫayr* 'Amen, amen, amen, may God reward you with all the best'.

Repetition is one of the crucial characteristics describing Arab communication in general. It might occur "at the phonological, morphological and lexical, syntactic, and semantic levels" (Feghali 1997: 358). It is central to Arab discourse, especially in an oral form (Johnstone Koch 1983). Also, the root repetition may seem somehow magical and persuasive, as in:
(449) *aḷḷāhumma farriğ humūm al-mahmūmīn* 'Oh, God, drive away the troubles of the troubled'.
(450) *rabbina yirḥamu bi raḥmitu* 'May our Lord have mercy on him [with his mercy]'.

In Egyptian as well as in other Arabic dialects the phenomenon of numerical multiplication is known and used to reinforce the message by multiplying the transmitted blessings. In the studied material, this phenomenon appeared in expressions appearing in the place of core I:
(451) *alf raḥma wi nūr ʿalēk ya ʿamm maḥmūd* '[A thousand] mercy and light for you uncle Maḥmūd'.

Specifically, in this example, *alf raḥma* is formulaic, and the numeral in it is not changeable, although many of these forms may leave room for variability. The same pattern is used in greetings, congratulating and other polite forms:
(452) *alf mabrūk* 'A thousand congratulations'.

Ferguson describes such numerical multiplications in Syrian Arabic, for instance, as a response to *marḥaba* 'hello' one may say: *marḥaba* 'hello', *marḥabtēn* 'two hellos', *mit marḥaba* 'a hundred hellos', *marāḥib* 'hellos'. He explains that "[t]his principle of response received endorsement in the Holy Koran itself, which says, in effect, (Surah IV, verse 86) 'If someone greets you, either return the greeting or greet him better, for God takes everything into account'" (Ferguson 1976: 144). However, as Ferguson himself points out, formulae intensified this way are conventional, so the method will not always be productive.

Another phenomenon related to the Arabic discursive style is the repetition of the same exchange of utterances over and over again in one meeting/speech event. It is a typical oral feature and in the current material it is found only in a rudimentary form. In the case of conversations about death and condolences, such repetition of consolation words and assurances about the deceased being in heaven characterises conversations between relatives. In this case, a single comment would be considered rude. The number of words matters, after all:

(453) (a) *aḷḷāh yirḥamu wi yigʿalu min ahl il-fardūs il-aʿla ya rabb in šāʾ aḷḷāh wi yiṣabbarkum ʿala furāʾu ya rabb in šāʾ aḷḷāh* 'May God have mercy on him and make him one of the inhabitants of the greatest garden, oh, Lord, God willing, and give you patience after the loss, oh, Lord, God willing'.
(b) *aḷḷāhumma amīn ya rabb* 'Oh, God, amen, oh, Lord'.
(a) *rabbina ya rabb yataqabbal min ḥaḍritik id-duʿāʾ wi yigazīki ḫēr wi yurzuʾik iṣ-ṣaḥḥa wi ṭūʿ il-ʿumr* 'May Lord accept your prayer and reward you well, and give you health and long life'.
(b) *aḷḷāhumma amīn ya rabb, aḷḷāhumma amīn* 'Oh, God, amen, oh, God, amen'.

However, in the present material the possibility of tracing this phenomenon is limited, because the relations between the speakers in most cases are unknown to the researcher. It is, nevertheless, important to note, that many of the features of the material discussed above resemble the oral variety of language. Orality, Johnstone Koch says, characterises "discourse that is patterned in a repetitive, paratactic, formulaic way" (1990: 215).

9. Death and the agency of God

In this section I will discuss a specific phenomenon of Arab (and Egyptian) culture, namely, the reference to God and his constant presence in human life. This theme is essentially related to the issues previously mentioned, and particularly to the relation between human fears and linguistic behaviour arising from them. The necessary element of this relation in Arab culture is supernatural agency: the relentless action of God and, on the other hand, his sinister powers. Considering the paucity of material on the linguistic behaviour of Egyptian Christians in the available literature, only references to Islam and Islamic values are made, which, of course, constitute a serious drawback and calls for more studies in the future.

In this section a term "positive transmission" will be used with reference to the idea of communication based on conveying blessing between interlocutors or evoking divine agency and help when it is needed in human life. This springs from the deeply rooted belief that *baraka* 'blessing' is an active power able to protect people from the sinister forces that are similarly active in the world. *Baraka* is believed to support people in their everyday endeavours and give them the power to overcome obstacles. Linguistic expressions with reference to God and his *baraka* are among the performative acts so, in other words, they are believed to have the power to change the state of affairs in human reality, whether social or spiritual. This section also partly discusses certain aspects of Arab culture that have an impact on the way they communicate. The first of these will be the specific way of seeing reality, which includes the humble acceptance of misfortune, the fact associated with the belief that human destiny is guided by God and nothing people do can change it.

9.1. Transmission of *baraka*

Baraka is a force present in the sacred words of the Quran (hence amulets containing Quranic passages) used for many different purposes (Hamady 1960: 167). It is a magical power, and yet constantly present in the everyday life of Egyptians as well as in their language. Many of the examples analysed here were of Quranic origin:

(454) *fī ğannātin wa nahr wa miqʿad ṣidqin malīkin muqtadir* 'In the midst of gardens and rivers in an assembly of truth, in the presence of a sovereign omnipotent'.

Stewart believes that the supernatural is for the Egyptians an "integral and even familiar participant in the events of daily life" (1996: 174). Language provides the link between the supernatural and the natural. The amount of *baraka* is gradable and can be augmented. Saints, for example, have an exceptional amount of it, which is why "domes are erected in places where they are buried, so that ordinary people can benefit from their powers of blessing" (Hamady 1960: 167). The transmission of *baraka* usually takes the form of a request addressed to God. The active verb is in the optative mood (either present or past, with the past seen as an archaic version) or imperative. Such transmission of *baraka* opens almost every interaction between Egyptians – a particularly large quantity of such formulae are spoken at the beginning of visits by relatives, especially when some time has elapsed since their last visit. In such cases, the greeting ceremony involves frequent and repeated blessing (asking God to bless others):

(455) *aḷḷāh maʿāk* 'God be with you'.

(456) *aḷḷāh yibārik fīk* 'God bless you'.

Some blessings might be extended, and therefore, enforced. One method of extension may include, for instance, the addition of *ʿumrak* 'your life' in place of the pronominal suffix: *aḷḷāh yibārik fīk* 'God bless you' > *aḷḷāh yibārik fi ʿumrak* 'God bless your life'. The insertion of *ʿumr* is "a polite counterpart to the common insult intensifiers *abu, ahl, dīn*, and so forth" (Stewart 1996: 165).

Transmitting *baraka* may be considered a multifunctional tool in the Egyptian politeness system. References to God appear in almost all situations when the taboo is involved. Whatever the problem, blessing seems to be the preferred way of manifesting concern, consolation, sympathy or gratitude. As far as the function of blessing is concerned, it usually realises the positive politeness strategies. In condolences, blessings are used to soothe the mourner by referring to the commonly held beliefs and rituals. When in danger, blessings involve requesting protection from God. Blessings accompany advice and thus soften or hedge a possible FTA. They can be seen as redressive actions, when direct on-record strategies are employed to convey tabooed or feared content.

Usually, the stronger the taboo, the greater the level of ritualisation, which results in more blessings. Blessings are also one of the most common ways of expressing thanks. They are also used to convey irony and are considered a polite way to show criticism.

Blessings and other references to God are found in every type of conversation; they are also plentiful. Almost every single conversation is spontaneously interwoven with blessings, *du'ā'* and other formulae. In terms of reacting to fear, whether the danger is real or not, courteous questions about the interlocutor's health and well-being are asked, often containing intensifiers and emotional vocabulary. *Baraka* is transmitted through frequent invocations addressed to God.

Blessings are not only abundant, but also further strengthened by terms of address (reinforcing the message by emphasising the intimacy of the relationship between the speakers and personalising the statements), repetition, breaking the Maxim of Quantity and numerical multiplication. When consoling a close friend, usually more than one formula is used at a time. With blessings, especially those with a future tense rather than the usual optative mood, the formula *in šā' aḷḷāh* 'God willing' or *bi izni ḷḷāh* 'with God's permission' is used lest the blessing bring the reverse. In the current material this is visible in:

(457) *fi l-ganna wa na'imha in šā' aḷḷāh* 'In heaven and its bliss, God willing'.
(458) *tkūn fi l-ganna in šā' aḷḷāh* 'May she be in heaven, God willing'.
(459) *fi gannāt in-na'īm bi izni ḷḷḷḷāh* 'In the garden of bliss, with God's permission'.

The *muṭlaq* construction is employed to intensify the meaning. Also, praising God as the possessor of required powers appears in this function:

(460) *yiṣabbarik ṣabran ǧamīlan* 'May [God] give you [beautiful] patience'.
(461) *huwwa l-munta'im il-gabbār* 'He is a mighty avenger'.

When answering blessings, the confirming response *ya rabb* 'oh, Lord' or *amīn* 'amen' is usually used. Egyptians tend to highlight the sincerity of their intention.

9.2. Islamic outlook on life

As Piamenta points out, the fatalistic outlook of Egyptians on life "deters the desire to lead, destroys an appreciation of the need for planning, impedes the spirit of inquiry, perpetuates an unbalanced attention to the spirit of other worldliness, and obstructs an appreciation of the value of time" (1979: 205). This view of life comes naturally from a deep conviction that no human intentions or plans can succeed without God's permission, command, and will. Hamady points out that the ideal Muslim should be disdainful and fatalistic, put all faith in God, accept his will with resignation and endure with equanimity and strength all misfortune (Hamady 1960: 199). Such a way of seeing things, however, may suggest unauthorised interpretations in a sphere of life not discussed in this work, e.g., politics, and therefore, it is important to emphasise that this book will always refer exclusively to the domain of linguistic behaviour.

According to Islam, every person is subject to the divine plan. Arabic expressions *qisma* and *naṣīb* refer to the 'portion', 'share' or 'lot' allotted man by God (Piamenta 1979: 188). *Qisma* comes from the verb meaning 'to share', whereas the verb *naṣaba* means 'to appoint', which refers to God's plans with respect to the individual. These expressions are used almost synonymously in various Arabic dialects. Both can have a pejorative meaning; *naṣīb* for instance, is often used in a negative semantic prosody, *mafīš naṣīb* is a polite way to reject a proposal. *Qisma* is sometimes used in a similar way:

(462) (a) *da ṭalab īdik minni il-lēla* 'This man asked me for your hand last night'.
(b) (dismissing her father with a flimsy excuse) *kulli šī 'isma wi naṣīb* 'Everything is a matter of appointed lot' (MP).

The phrase "it's *qisma*" is used as an explanation for the misfortune afflicting man, for example having many daughters but no sons, the loss of money or land, the death of a loved one, health deterioration. It is said then:

(463) *rabbina 'āyiz kida* 'Our Lord wishes it so' (MP).
(464) *'ismiti kida* 'This is my fate' (MP).
(465) *šūf il-'isma* 'Look at my fate' (MP).

A popular saying illustrates the relationship of the human arrangements to the divine will:

(466) *ana bi t-tafkīr, aḷḷāh bi t-tadbīr* 'I propose, God disposes' (MP),

or another version of the same saying:

(467) *il-'abd bi t-tafkīr, wi r-rabb fi t-tadbīr* 'A servant proposes and God disposes' (MP).

Fate, destiny, and allotment are often understood as a text written by God, so:

(468) *il-maktūb maktūb, maḥaddiš ḍāmin min 'umru yōm* 'Whatever is allotted is destined. No one can guarantee one day of one's life' (MP).
(469) *kull illi l-maktūb 'ala l-gibīn lāzim il-'ēn tišūfu* 'Whatever is written on the forehead, one's eye[s] shall see' (MP).

Piamenta (1979: 147) explains two similar concepts of *qaḍā'* and *qadar*, saying that *qaḍā'* means 'general decree of God' applicable for everything that lives, whereas *qadar* is a 'particular decree of God' and refers to a person defining his/her birth, life and death. Both concepts refer to the predestination of fate and destiny, thus shaping the Arab manner of perceiving reality that is often defined in Western literature as "fatalism" or the subordination of the individual to the will of God.

At the same time, a man wants to be freed from his/her fate, often associated with negative experiences (*ibid.*). Arabs believe it is impossible, there is no escape from the divine will, which should be accepted with humility:

(470) *ʿumr il-ḥazar mabyimnaʿ ʾadar* 'Never can caution prevent fate' (MP).

(471) *quddira fa kān* 'The inevitable happened' (MP).

(472) *kull illi mʾaddaru ʿalēna kuwayyis* 'Whatever he decrees on us is good' (MP).

Therefore, such reactions to death, disaster or misfortune as presented below are not uncommon in the spoken language:

(473) *qaḍāʾ wi qadar* 'It's a fate and destiny' (MP).

(474) *amr aḷḷāh* 'It's God's order' (MP).

(475) *qaḍāʾ rabbina* 'It's our Lord's decree' (MP).

Fate is unknown to man, and, as often highlighted, it must be accepted:

(476) (a) *ya ʿālam, mīn ʿārif hayiḥṣal ēh bukra?* 'Everybody! Who knows what is going to happen [tomorrow]?' (MP).
(b) *kull šī bi amr aḷḷāh* 'Everything is God's decree' (MP).

In accordance with the dictates of Islam one should believe that God's plan is perfect, even if it is incomprehensible or turns out to be cruel:

(477) *rabbina yigīb il-ʿawāʾib is-salīma* 'May our Lord make the end safe!' (MP).

For the Arab, God is omniscient, and he is the only one to know all past and future events, because human knowledge cannot be compared with his knowledge; God is also infallible, free from negligence and error (Piamenta 1979: 185). At the same time, human knowledge is limited, and human nature leads him/her to weakness and failure. A human being must acknowledge his/her ignorance at every step, lest he/she claim for him-/herself the right to what is reserved for God: *iḏa suʾiltum ʿamma lā taʿlamūna ... taqūlūna aḷḷāhu aʿlam* 'if you are asked about something you do not know, you say "God knows best"' (*ibid.*):

(478) (a) *huwwa l-bāša hayitʾaḫḫar?* 'Will the Pasha be late?'
(b) *subḥān il-ʿālim* 'Praise [God] the Knower!' (MP).

The following expression was uttered in reaction to misfortune:

(479) *aḷḷāh lā yiʾaddir* 'May God not decree [it]! (MP).

It is to be understood rather as a request to God to dismiss the danger. When finally relieved from danger, people express their gratitude to God:

(480) *ʾaḍḍa wi laṭaf* 'He predestined and was kind' (MP).

According to Islamic beliefs, whatever happens in the world, happens by divine permission (*iḏn*). Men can plan and execute their intentions only when God wishes them to happen:

(481) *ḥimlit bi izni ḷḷāh wi kammilit it-tisʿat ušhur* 'She became pregnant, by God's permission, and completed the nine months' (MP).

(482) (a) *il-ḥāla yiẓhar hidyit* 'The situation seems to be calm now'.
(b) *hadya bi izni ḷḷāh* 'It is calm, God willing' (MP).

For an Egyptian, nothing happens beyond the knowledge and permission of God: "God's 'leave' or 'permission' for man to act (and for this purpose, for events to occur) implying God's withdrawal or removal of prevention or prohibition, and the giving of power and ability, concomitant with the opinion that the action of men are by their own effective power but facilitated by God – implies the subordination of actions and events to the will of God, to his command and decree" (Piamenta 1979: 183). God's command (*amr, zukm*) is a Quranic concept of defining the boundaries of human activity. According to the Quran, Heaven and Earth were created out of God's order and whatever God commands becomes the destiny of man (Piamenta 1979: 182). The following example illustrates the action of God's will (*ʾirāda*); the expression was used in order to console a man on the birth of a daughter:

(483) *di irādit rabbina* 'This is our Lord's decree' (MP).

In turn, the following is used as an expression of resignation in the face of unwanted obligation (Piamenta 1979: 197):

(484) *amri li ḷḷāh* 'I give up' (MP).

At the same time the good and the beautiful is also the result of divine will. The exclamation *mā šāʾ aḷḷāh* (*ma šāʾ aḷḷāh*) 'God wished it so' is used to express admiration, as well as congratulations:

(485) *ma šāʾ aḷḷāh* 'God wished it so'.

(486) *subḥān aḷḷāh* 'Praise be to God'.

In šāʾ aḷḷāh 'God willing' is perhaps the ultimate example of Arab fatalism; it is a reminder that every future event and every single human step depend on the will of God.

(487) (a) *iwʿa tinsa* 'Do not forget!'
(b) *lā in šāʾ aḷḷāh* 'No, God willing' (MP).

The Egyptian above all hopes that what God sends is good; the expression *ḫēr in šāʾ aḷḷāh* 'God willing, it's good' is typically used in moments of apprehension, anxiousness or indiscreetness (because of someone's incomprehensible behaviour) in order to express the hope that what God sends is nevertheless good for man (Piamenta 1979: 218). When a child gets hurt and cries, parents usually console him/her with:

(488) *ḥaṣal ḥēr* 'It's nothing [good thing happened]'.

10. The taboo of death

Everyday human exchange poses a number of threats to the social image of the interactants (Brown and Levinson 1987), therefore, a number of restrictions are imposed on people navigating the gamut of daily interactions with other members of the community. Such restrictions may be equated with taboos in which some modes of behaviour, actions or utterances are seen as prohibited. The nature of such taboo exchange is two-fold: on the one hand, it may be a source of benefit or blessing, while on the other hand, it brings danger and causes apprehension. Linguistic interaction in the Arab world may be summed up as: avoiding the evil through recourse to God and seeking the good in every speech moment, which is also achieved through requests directed to God. Blessing and danger are both transmitted in language. Elements of language (words and expressions) are the media carrying what brings luck or misfortune. Positive and negative transmissions are two aspects of communication that can be distinguished in the linguistic exchange, both of which bring a number of ritual behaviours involving a resort to God. People seek *baraka* 'blessing' for themselves and their surroundings as a necessary element of life. For dangerous situations, a number of avoidance strategies are found in communication forming a stable and conventionalised system. A similar point of view is presented by Piamenta:

> Every created thing is far from being neutral in respect of man, but it has in it a dual aspect, an active principle of good and an active principle of evil. The common form of *isti'ādha* in regard to this is: *as'aluka khayra (hu) wa-'a'ūdhu bika min sharri (h)*, 'I ask Thee for the good of (it) and I take refuge with Thee from the evil of (it)'. Sometimes though only refuge with God from the evil of it mentioned (1979: 96).

Potentially, every situation presents an element of good and evil. In certain situations, when an Arab is involved in a form of danger (taboo), he/she pronounces a formula designed to ensure that he/she would experience only the positive aspects of it. Such utterances are usually invocations addressed to God or Quranic formulae thought to possess magical powers. These might include:

(489) *aḷḷāhumma innī as'aluka ḫayrahā wa a'ūḏu bika min šarrihā* 'Oh, God! I ask Thee for the good of her/him/it and I take refuge with Thee from the evil of her/him/it' (MP).

The analysis of the material presented earlier shows that it fits in with what was aforementioned regarding the taboo: when speaking about death and responding to a death announcement, people refer to God asking him for mercy, forgiveness and a place in heaven for the deceased, as well as for patience for the mourner. In doing so, they use a number of formulae, while novel language is very rarely seen in such exchanges. Of the wide range of ritual forms (presented earlier) which are used in times of uncertainty, danger and stress, the following are employed in relation to death: *ismalla, tahlīl, istirǧā', ḥawqala,* and *taḫliyya.* Creativity, if exercised at all, manifests itself in rare (though still formulaic) expressions, quoting prayers, Hadiths, and the Quran. In this context, several important questions arise. What is the origin of tendency towards formulaicity in reaction to the taboo of death? Why are so few comments linguistically novel? Coulmas argues that the primary function of the formulaic sequences, which he calls routine formulae, is "to reduce the complexity of social interaction" (1979: 254). Coulmas gives an accurate explanation as to why such routines occur:

> In every given social situation every participant has to decide whether he can and wants to achieve a change of that situation, and further, what means he would have to employ in order to occasion the intended change. Situations differ with respect to their continuation patterns and the significance of every communicative act is relative to that pattern, insofar as it conforms to or violates the pattern. There are, occasionally, "vague" situations with no obvious pattern; no typification facilitates the decision finding process. Such situations are likely to produce stress or awkward feelings in the participants. They feel helpless and literally don't know what to say. In Western cultures situations of this kind often occur in connection with such tabooed matters as death or sexual maturation. Other cultures avert behavioural uncertainty in these contexts by relying on initiation and mourning rites (*ibid.*).

The author adds that the use of formulae is to ensure that the exact message the speaker intended is conveyed.

As previously mentioned, one of the reasons why formulae are used instead of novel language is the economy of effort. Perkins says it accounts for the "prevalence of formulaicity in the adult language system" (1999: 56). It saves effort required in language production by providing linguistic scaffolding for the recurrent situations in our everyday experience. But how does this saving of effort become apparent in taboo situations related to death? Wray (2002) explains this and other phenomena observed in connection with the use of formulae looking beyond the linguistic dependencies. In line with her claim, formulaicity relates to the economy of effort in the context of resources available to the speaker allowing for the encoding and decoding of information in situations when there are some circumstances that might impede this process (see: Coulmas' view above). Wray says: "understanding a spoken message in a noisy room or during an emotionally charged exchange will normally make greater demands on the listener than will a casual conversation. If the demands are too great, then the individual will not be able to engage in all the complex processing that the situation requires" (2002: 15).

In accordance with dual processing model, by processing information and producing sentences, human brain activates two mechanisms that operate simultaneously depending on the need: it generates novel sentences or uses prefabricates. The question is: on what basis is this choice made? Wray offers one of the possible answers, if "processing pressures are abnormally high" (2002: 17) the speaker tends to choose formulae rather than novel language. This can be determined by physical obstacles or the requirements of politeness and delicacy in interaction with another person. This usually happens when we talk to someone who has lost a loved one. The context of death marks the situation in a particular way. Both the speaker and the recipient of the message may be under stress. For the one who suffered a loss, social interactions may trigger a highly emotional response. On the other hand, for the interlocutor the need to behave in a delicate way may be a source of uncertainty about the choice of language that is appropriate to the situation. At the same time, the conversation requires that the intentions of the speaker are easy to interpret by the recipient.

Researchers have long observed that stress affects the way people formulate their thoughts and their ability to understand. Experimental studies show that under severe stress, the language produced by healthy people may resemble aphasic-like language (Wray and Perkins 2000:17). When under stress, people refer to formulaicity because the human mind cannot cope with it and needs ready-made templates. This reduces unnecessary ambiguity and possible communication errors that lead to misunderstanding. Therefore, formulae make communication easier; no danger of committing an FTA pertains. Another important thing is that the formulaic language allows for unambiguity. As related by Coulmas, formulae "represent petrified forms of typical behavior for handling certain types of situations. The decision finding process for continuing these situations is predetermined. Interactants can rely on societal knowledge incarnated in the verbal means for routinized speech behavior" (1979: 251). How does this happen? Probably through their acquisition in specific situational conditions, formulae gain multidimensional semantic scope and often apply to the entire cultural concept. The routinisation and repetitiveness of formulae in a specific contextual environment leads to their embedding in various situations encountered in life. This endows them with multi-layer symbolism which is based on the shared knowledge of community members. Formulae, understood this way are a part of both linguistic and cultural competences. They allow interactants "to direct their attention to the larger structure of the discourse, rather than keeping it focused narrowly on individual words as they are produced" (Wray 2002, quoting Nattinger and DeCarrico 1992: 32). According to Wray avoiding problems with encoding/decoding of information is possible because formulae "offer social support to deal with situations that are awkward or stressful . . . (and) make communication more orderly because they are regulatory in nature. They organize reactions and facilitate choices, thus reducing the complexity of communicative exchanges" (2002: 52). The evidence that the formulaicity affects the speed of information transfer and decoding as well as their disambiguation comes from the previously described neurolinguistic studies which became the basis of the mentioned dual processing model. The conducted experiments prove that newly created language is modulated by the left hemisphere, while the responsibility for formulaic language lies in right hemisphere/subcortical circuit (Van Lancker Sidtis 2012b). Therefore, this kind of "automatic speech" forms what can be referred to as right hemisphere language – expressions retrieved from the memory impromptu, which does not involve grammatical processing. This kind of language is strongly related to context and often almost ritualised and so requires little processing. It is often preserved in people with severe aphasia due to left hemisphere lesions. Such people sometimes produce sentences that are correct in terms of articulation and prosody (Van Lancker Sidtis 2012a). The premises linking right-hemispheric language with "appreciation of social and linguistic context" (p. 350) also come from neurolinguistic studies. Reactions to death announcements and condolences are similar to gestures in that they are not about conveying information, but emotions. Basal ganglia/limbic system are responsible for formulaic language and also take part in the regulation of motor and emotional behaviour. In addition, as the author notes, these areas are also attributed the "acquisition and execution of gestures that are compatible with processing of formulaic expressions" (Van Lancker Sidtis 2012a: 355). Researchers also recognise the similarity of formulaic sequences to animal calls (Van Lancker Sidtis 2012a, Wray 2000), whose function is to facilitate inter-group interaction. Van Lancker Sidtis adds: "Similarly, some formulaic language in humans, such as swearing and other interjections, are likely mediated by limbic system structures and, presumably, were originally intended to perform the social functions of repulsing intruders and expressing anger and dissatisfaction" (2012a: 355). The areas in question are sometimes called the "old brain". Van Lancker Sidtis continues to conclude that "the older system may continue to perform, in ways only partially understood, in singing and in emotional and routinized vocal behaviors" (2012a: 356).

The formulae that appear in response to the taboo of death are regulated by the areas of the brain responsible for reacting to the situation with which they are related through lifelong experience. Why is this beneficial to us humans? Speaking under stress can make communication awkward and ineffective. It might be simply easier to convey emotional support in a symbolic, undemanding manner that is easy to produce and read. In this respect, the three groups of formulae examined here: death announcements, reactions to death and dialogues, differ to some degree. The first one stands out because of the fact that it is significantly less formulaic, which can be explained by the informative element present in the death announcements. Above all, the convey information, while the other two communicate emotions.

Wray proposes considering what would happen if we used novel language in place of formulaic phrases in certain situations. What if a person wishing to quietly escape a meeting uses some kind of non-formulaic sentence instead of just "excuse me"? Wray concludes that: "When someone says *Excuse me* as they stand up or move away, the intention is an unobtrusive apology, which can be registered without any interruption to the main event. Using a novel utterance like *It's time for me to leave now* would require the hearer to pay more attention to the words, and so it would be more invasive" (2002: 95). In the next example the situational requirement concerns managing a large group of people. If the army were to use non-formulaic phrases, interpreted individually by each person, instead of orders, there would be chaos and disorganisation. Formulaicity helps to convey exactly what is intended; it gives the speaker the ability to control the message sent. It also allows the recipient to narrow down the possibilities of interpretation.

In her explanations of the role of formulaicity, Wray refers to the theory of relevance (Sperber and Wilson 1987/1996: 474), which assumes that the speaker chooses a way of speaking that will involve the least possible effort to convey the intended message (Wray 2002). The use of formula fits with certain normative mode of behaviour and is interpreted based on what both speakers agree on in terms of beliefs. The conventionality of formulae lies in their predetermined meaning, for they are both unambiguous and easily interpretable. An additional benefit of using a routine form in response to taboos is that it does not require an elaborate and adequate response from the sufferer. In fact, in Egypt it does not require any answer at all. Typically, the time after losing a loved one is filled with loneliness, which is intentional. In such cases, considerations of politeness steer the speaker towards showing compassion, while limiting impositions. It can be seen in the material, only about ¼ of the comments examined here received any answer at all, of which the vast majority was conventional, not going beyond the routine formula. Wray adds "In all of these manipulative expressions, it is in the speaker's interests to ensure that the hearer understands, since the intended effect of the utterance is to create a situation beneficial to the speaker: it also serves its own manipulative function, by inviting the hearer to perceive you as polite" (2002: 95).

The taboo responses presented in this book have been analysed and interpreted in accordance with the theory proposed by Wray, which, however, presents an even broader view on formulaicity. It collapses many different benefits of using formulaicity into one that is non-linguistic in nature, as Wray (2002: 95) says: "[o]n closer consideration, it becomes clear that *all* of the functions of formulaic sequences that have been identified (...) actually serve a single goal: the promotion of the speaker's interests." Researchers studying interpersonal interactions (Goffman 1967; Brown and Levinson 1987) have long concluded that normative behaviour is aimed at promoting the "self" (both of the speaker and the interlocutor), and thus, in a broader perspective, they help maintaining correct relations in society and a sense of security in all its members.

The theory referred here presents the formulae used in response to the taboo of death in a new light, as it combines their tabooness with formulaicity. Within this framework, the creativity that interlocutors demonstrate lies in most cases in the selection of formulae. On the one hand, the very conventional *aḷḷāh yirḥamu* 'may God have mercy on him' may be enough, but if the participants of the conversation are close to each other, the utterance may adopt a highly exuberant form and quotes of Quranic verses, Hadiths and prayers may be invoked. On the other hand, another scenario is also possible in such a situation where simple blessings covering the most conventional formulae found in all slots (see: Table 1), and "amen" responses are repeated several times in subsequent turns of the conversation. In this way, the conversation may continue without any reference to novel language. From the point of view of politeness, it is a successful and safe (in terms of face) for both interactants. The safety of this type of interaction consists in the fact that none of the participants experience awkwardness and there is no risk of misunderstanding any intentions.

The fact that formulae are so ubiquitous and obligatory is determined by cultural considerations and conventions in the society under examination. Egyptians, due to their cultural collectivism, value communal cohesion above all (Khalid 1977: 127). Social institutions in Egypt strengthen and confirm the legitimacy of the operative norms and values at every step (Feghali 1997). Child rearing methods based on shame and strong subordination to vertical relations in the community and in the family serve this purpose (Feghali 1997). Also, "subject matter codes" as Pawley (1991: 339) calls them depend on cultural conventions. They determine *what* is said and *how* in a given community. Therefore, not only *how* people say things matters, but also what kind of ideas they express and what concepts they ignore. What kind of content should be conveyed in a given communicative situation? In the case of reactions to death, it concerns in a broad sense religious belief and the idea of referring to God. However, "subject matter codes" also apply to very small details of speaking, such as for instance the already mentioned act of transferring blessing to the entire Muslim community while asking God for mercy for the deceased person. The same happens when cursing someone; the intention might be for the curse to cover all wrong doers of a similar kind. Wray (2002) explains that it is only through such cultural conventions that we are able to at least partially answer the question of why certain grammatical strings are valid and used in a given community, while others might be absent altogether.

11. Summary

In this book the analysis of utterances sent over Facebook on the occasion of death was presented. The analysis of the material brings us to the conclusion that death in Egyptian society is a phenomenon dealt with indirectly; the picture is mediated by religion and beliefs. When responding to an announcement about someone's death, Egyptians most often use blessings. They ask God to provide the mourner with patience and to grant the deceased a place in heaven. The solace of blessings is based on faith in the power of divine grace (*baraka*).

Baraka 'divine grace' is considered to operate in the life of Muslims at every moment and in all their endeavours. The transmission of *baraka* is one of the basic rituals of everyday polite exchange in Arab culture. According to Hamady (1960: 77–78) conveying blessing is a regular part of a broad complex of ritual greetings exchanged during visits; this involves requests addressed to God for the interlocutor's health, long living and well-being: "God bless you", "God multiply those who resemble you", "God recompense you" (for thanks) are some examples of such expressions (*ibid.*). God is a constant agent in human life. His omnipresence is attested and referred to even in the most mundane activities of daily life. God is regarded as a source of power (*quwwa, ḥawl*). It is believed that all past, current and future human activity is carried out purely by the power of the divine that is granted to people, hence the expression: *rabbina ʾaddarni* 'God gave me the power [to do something]' A person often refers to God while asking for his active participation in their life. Daily interaction includes a request for blessing at every opportunity, recourse to God in moments of horror and danger, and sometimes requests for misery to befall enemies, e.g., curse.

In this book, a response to the taboo of death was studied based on the CMC data gathered from Facebook. A randomly selected group of 20 death announcements, 857 comments and 220 turns of dialogues were analysed in terms of their formulaicity. Additionally, the group of comments was also examined quantitively to provide a general structural pattern of response to death announcements on Facebook.

It was found that death announcements were mostly non-formulaic and no repetitive pattern was established for such a genre. However, no conclusion can be drawn with such scant data. On the other hand, the analysis of comments and dialogues showed recurrent patterns in both these groups. A typical comment may resemble the following:

(490) *inna li ḷḷāh wa inna ilayhi ragiʿūn, rabbina yirḥamu wi ġfirlu wi yinawwar ʾabru wi yiskinu l-fardūs il-aʿla, wi yiṣabbar ʿalbik ya ḥabibti* 'Verily to God we belong and unto him is our return, may our Lord have mercy on him and forgive him, and illuminate his grave, and make him live in the greatest paradise, and soothe your heart, my love'.

It starts with a formula introducing the theme of death and transferring the conversation into a territory sanctified by customs and religious considerations. Then the speaker asks God for mercy (1), and forgiveness for the deceased. The next supplication is that he/she may receive a place in heaven. Lastly the speaker turns his/her attention to the mourner and asks God to give him/her patience and peace of heart. The whole sequence partially runs according to the pattern summarised below. The intensity of grey indicates the frequency with which a given formula occurs in the material. In the example (505) the utterance might have started with an opening formula consisting of a religious expression of a broader sense, e.g., the Shahada. It might also have been rounded off with the repetition of one of the first formulae – named here closing and framing formulae:

opening formula 10.3%	framing formula 11.7%	core I 73.4%	core II 43.9%	supplement I 43%	supplement II 24.1%	framing formula 1.4%	closing formula 0.5%

Figure 2. The percentage of occurrences in particular slots

Between the slots distinguished here discourse markers appear including invocation *ya rabb* 'oh, Lord', the vocative particle *ya* with personal names, terms of endearment and a few other items.

In terms of dialogues, three patterns were most often encountered: duplets, triplets and quadruplets. The conventional response to the condoler is *amīn* 'amen' or *aḷḷāhumma amīn* 'oh, God, amen', although additional elements often appear. Some of the dialogues end here, but most of them are continued to include one more turn, usually *rabbina yataqabbal minnak/ik id-duʿā* 'may our Lord accept your prayer'. There were a few examples of four-turn dialogues:

(491) (a) *aḷḷāh yirḥamu ḥabībi* 'May our Lord have mercy on him'.
(b) *aḷḷāhumma amīn ya rabb rabbina yiḥallīk* 'Oh, God, amen, oh, Lord, may our Lord keep you safe'.

(492) (a) *rabbina yirḥamu wi yiskinu il-fardūs il-aʿla* 'May our Lord have mercy on him and make him live in the greatest garden'.
(b) *aḷḷāhumma amīn ya rabb* 'Oh, God, amen, oh, Lord'.
(a) *rabbina yataqabbal minnik id-duʿā ya rabb ḥabibti* 'May our Lord accept your prayer, oh, Lord, my dear'.

(493) (a) *rabbina yirḥamu raḥma wasʿa wi yiṣabbarik* 'May Lord have [great] mercy on him and give you patience'.
(b) *aḷḷāhumma amīn ya rabb* 'Oh, God, amen, oh, Lord'.
(a) *rabbina yiʿawwiḍik ḫēr ya rabb* 'May our Lord compensate it for you well'.
(b) *il-ḥamdu li llāh ʿala kulli šī* 'Praise be to God for everything'.

In the material a few methods of intensification of blessings occur. They are mostly lexical or based on repetition and the number of formulae used:

(494) *aḷḷāhumma rzuʾu fūʾ in-naʿīm naʿīm* 'Oh, God, bestow upon him bliss that is beyond all blisses'.

In the material a great number of utterances have an exuberant character and a strongly emotional tone. Different expressions are combined to strengthen the effect. Intense and effusive displays of affection through positive politeness are used to maximise the message. Blessings are multiplied and many repetitions appear based on an assumption that more form equals more content. The elaboration and the use of intensifiers maximises the consolation and gives it cathartic powers. Repetitions are frequent both at the level of utterance as well as interaction. Invocation to God involving repetition may be single or multi-authored and consist of blessings or elements of *duʿāʾ*. Supernatural and mystical speech acts such as prayers are a common strategy. When nonconventional expressions appear, it is usually to communicate to the mourner the sincerity of speaker.

Prayers, poetic attempts, excerpts of Quran and Hadith consist of prefabricates memorised and retrieved from the memory similarly to items from a dictionary. Regulated by right hemisphere of the brain, they are closely related to other aspects of communication: context, emotionality and pragmatics. Formulae function discursively like symbols, they denote complex cultural concepts by relating to multi-layered and multi-dimensional situations that happen regularly in life. Formulaicity is a crucial feature of the response to the taboo of death in Egyptian Arabic. Particularly when comments and dialogues are considered, it appears that the whole discourse is very uniform, which might be motivated by "the desire to sound like others in the speech community" (Wray 2002). Further analysis proposes perceiving the formulaicity in the material as related to the tabooness of the topic and the stress triggered by it. Using formulaic instead of novel language allows the speaker to communicate emotional support in a conventional manner that is easy to decode. It also allows for the removal of any ambiguity that might otherwise creep in if the speaker were to use entirely new linguistic structures, while being under stress.

Nevertheless, the results presented here cannot be generalised to apply to the whole discourse about death in Egyptian Arabic. Firstly, only three types of communicative acts have been discussed here, all of which appear almost exclusively on social media. The language of CMC has its own characteristics which might influence linguistic production. When it comes to the language of the Internet, it seems that more sophisticated formulae are used, which is probably more pronounced in the production of those speakers who are sensitive to the prestigious aspects of language. The written form facilitates unusual linguistic production, which is even easier with the help of search engines and ready-made patterns. Furthermore, prayers, condolences and other formulae are widespread throughout the Internet and multiplied freely, which leads to the possible emergence in the material of linguistic items used in other Arabic regions. The use of literary Arabic has several functions, some of which include refinement of speech by reference to the religion and religious culture, mediating the everyday experience and thus creating distance between people and their suffering as well as providing a context for human emotions. Often, particularly in the case of highly conventional forms, the MSA or even CA forms are dialectalised to a greater or lesser extent; all of the following forms are possible: *rabbina yiṣabbarku* (EA), *rabbina yiṣabbarkum* (mixed, the most common) and *aḷḷāh yuṣabbirukum* (the least frequent, MSA). When the example is provided in Arabic script, which happens in most cases, the context does not allow for a clear distinction as to which form was used.

12. Questions for further exploration

Due to its size, the work presented here very briefly tackles some of the problems that arise during analysis and therefore issues that require further research in the future should be summarised. In this respect, linguistic issues come to the fore, in particular those related to the use of mixed variety. A thorough study of formulae taking into account phonetic realisation as well as variation in the choice of classical or dialectal items along with their situational and contextual determinants is called for. Nevertheless, this cannot be achieved with the type of data analysed here; instead, it would require a sizeable corpus of spontaneous oral utterances gathered in an inobtrusive way, which obviously poses a considerable challenge to the researcher.

Other problems are more directly related to the type of data used here. A problematic issue is the "third party factor" in CMC, mentioned previously, leading to the numerous acts of self-presentation and an exceptional attentiveness to the form of the verbal production posted online. This situation also causes some other linguistic phenomena that were not discussed exhaustively in this work. One of them is the "emblematic" role of the standard variety and its development in CMC. It is assumed that at least some speakers have a poor command of MSA, yet they use this variety frequently in their online posts. Therefore, it would be of great importance to examine the language used by them in the context of linguistic correctness, and perhaps, language change.

Other issues concern typically Arabic manners of expression, an example of which is the role and pragmatic function of adjuration. Adjuration in EA is used in all types of conversations, strengthening the message and conveying the sincerity of speaker. It can be considered as a specifically Arabic act in everyday verbal exchanges. However, it does not appear in situations involving strong taboo like death. Investigating this issue might contribute greatly to the analysis of emotionality of Arabic speech.

Ferguson argues, "[t]he obligatory inclusion of a God-wish in response to a health inquiry, however, seems of sufficient regularity and the linguistic conditions of its occurrence so readily stable, that it would seem to belong within the grammar. Similarly for the replay pattern of greeting exchanges" (1997a: 224). As we could see, a great number of examples in this study were based on so called "magical powers of language", they include blessings, curses, etc. Some of them are fixed expressions and are no longer felt to involve supernatural agency, but many others do. Therefore, defining the level of semantic satiation of such linguistic forms is a problem requiring further investigation.

Finally, the kind of research presented in this work involved the Muslim element of Egyptian society only. More studies are required, which should encompass Christians as well, as they represent a considerable proportion of the Egyptian population.

Bibliography

Abdalla, M.A. (2009). *Translating English Euphemisms Into Arabic: Challenges and Strategies.* American University of Sharjah: unpublished master's thesis.

Abdel Samad, F. (1990). *Politeness strategies in spoken British English and spoken Egyptian Arabic. A contrastive Study.* Cairo University: doctoral dissertation.

Abdou, A. (2010) *The Semantic Structure of Arabic Idioms.* [In:] *Perspectives on Formulaic Language, Acquisition and Communication.* Ed. D. Wood. London–New York: Continuum, 234–256.

Aijmer, K. (1996). *Conversational Routines in English.* London–New York: Longman.

Al-Hamad M.Q. and Salman A.M. (2013). *The Translatability of Euphemism in The Holy Quran.* "European Scientific Journal", 9 (2). http://eujournal.org/index.php/esj/article/view/723. Access: April 2021.

Al-Khatib, M.A. and Salem, Z. (2011). *Obituary Announcements in Jordanian and British Newspapers: A Cross-Cultural Overview.* "Acta Linguistica", 5 (2), 80–96. https://core.ac.uk/download/pdf/270252659.pdf. Access: July 2021.

Allan, K. and Burridge, K. (2006). *Forbidden Words. Tabu and the Censoring of Language.* Cambridge: Cambridge University Press.

Al-Marrani, Y. and Sazalie, A. (2010). *Polite Request Strategies by Male Speakers of Yemeni Arabic in Male-Male Interaction and Male-Female Interaction.* "The International Journal of Language Society and Culture", 30, 63–80.

Al-Qahtani, H.A. (2009). *Female Use of Politeness Strategies in the Speech Act of Offering: A Contrastive Study between Spoken Saudi Arabic and Spoken British English.* King Saud University: unpublished master's thesis.

Ameka, F. (1987). *A comparative analysis of linguistic routines in two languages: English & Ewe.* "Journal of Pragmatics", (11), 299–326.

Aubed, M.M. (2012). *Polite Requests in English and Arabic: A Comparative Study.* „Theory and Practice in Language Studies", 2(5), 916–922.

Austin, J. (1962). *How to Do Things with Words.* Oxford: Oxford University Press.

Badarneh, M.A. (2020). *Formulaic Expressions of Politeness in Jordanian Arabic Social Interactions.* [In:] *Formulaic Language and New Data Theoretical and Methodological Implications.* Eds. E. Piirainen, N. Filatkina, S. Stumpf, C. Pfeiffer. Berlin, Boston: De Gruyter, 151–170.

Badawi, S.M. (1973). *Mustawayāt al-luġa al-ʿarabiyya al-muʿāṣira.* Cairo: Dār al-maʿārif.

Badawi, S.M. and Hinds, M. (1986). *A dictionary of Egyptian Arabic, Arabic-English.* Beirut: Librarie du Liban.

Bani Mofarrej, O.M., and Al-Haq, F.A. (2015). *A Sociolinguistic Study of Euphemistic Death Expressions in Jordanian Arabic.* "Arab World English Journal" (AWEJ), 6 (2), 110–130.

Biber, D. (1988). *Variation Across Speech and Writing.* Cambridge: Cambridge University Press.

Bobrow, S. and Bell, S. (1973). *On catching on to idiomatic expressions.* "Memory & Cognition", 1 (3), 343–346.

Brown, P. and Levinson, S. (1987). *Politeness: Some Universals in Language Usage.* Cambridge: Cambridge University Press.

Collot, M. and Belmore, N. (1996). *Electronic language: A new variety of English.* [In:] *Computer-mediated communication: Linguistic, social, and cross-cultural perspectives.* Ed. S.C. Herring. Amsterdam: John Benjamins.

Coulmas, F. (1979). *On the Sociolinguistic Relevance of Routine Formulae.* "Journal of Pragmatics", 3 (3), 239–266.

Crystal, D. (2001). *Language and the Internet.* Cambridge: Cambridge University Press.

Danecki, J. (2003). *Gniew Boga w islamie. Anatomia gniewu.* [In:] *Emocje negatywne w językach i kulturach świata.* A. Duszak and N. Pawlak (red.). Warszawa: Wydawnictwa Uniwersytetu Warszawskiego.

D'Anna, L. (2014). *Some aspects of verbal politeness in Maghrebi Arabic dialects.* Università degli studi di Napoli "L'Orientale": unpublished doctoral dissertation.

Dorleijn, M. (2016). *Introduction: Using Multilingual Written Internet Data in Code-Switching and Language Contact Research.* "Journal of Language Contact", 9 (1), 5–22.

Douglas, M. (1966). *Purity and Danger. An Analysis of Concepts of Pollution and Taboo.* London: Routledge & Kegan Paul.

El Shazly, A. (1994). *Requesting strategies in American English, Egyptian Arabic and English as spoken by Egyptian second language learners.* American University in Cairo: unpublished doctoral thesis. https://fount.aucegypt.edu/retro_etds/1000. Access: July 2021.

Elserafy, A. and Arseven, S. (2013). Politeness, directness and honorifics in Egyptian Arabic and Turkish requests: A cross-cultural study. "EDULEARN13 Proceedings", 3569–3574.

Fahmi Bataineh, R. (2013). *On Congratulating, Thanking, and Apologizing in Jordanian Arabic and American English.* "Journal of Intercultural Communication", 32. http://www.immi.se/intercultural/nr32/bataineh.html. Access: July 2021.

Farahat, S.H. (2009). *Politeness phenomena in Palestinian Arabic and Australian English. A cross-cultural study of selected contemporary plays.* Australian Catholic University: unpublished doctoral thesis.

Feghali, E. (1997). *Arab Cultural Communication Patterns.* "International Journal of Intercultural Relations", 21 (3), 345–378.
Ferguson, C. (1959). *Diglossia.* "Word", (15), 325–340.
Ferguson, C. (1976). *The Structure and Use of Politeness Formulas.* "Language in Society", 5 (2), 137–151.
Ferguson, C. (1997a). *God wishes in Syrian Arabic.* [In:] *Structuralist Studies in Arabic Linguistics.* Eds. K. Belnap and N. Haeri. Brill, 212–228.
Ferguson, C. (1997b). *Root-Echo Response in Syrian Arabic.* [In:] *Structuralist Studies in Arabic Linguistics.* Eds. K. Belnap and N. Haeri. Brill, 198–205.
Ferguson, C. (1997c). *The blessing of the Lord be upon you.* [In:] *Structuralist Studies in Arabic Linguistics.* Eds. K. Belnap and N. Haeri. Brill, 206–211.
Frazer, J. G. (1911). *The Golden Bough. A Study in Magic and Religion,* vol. III, part II *(Taboo and the Perils of the Soul).* London: MacMillan and Co.
Freud, S. (1918). *Totem and Taboo.* New York: Moffat, Yard.
Goffman, E. (1967). *Interaction ritual: Essays in face-to-face behavior.* Chicago: Aldine Pub. Co.
Gomaa, Y.A. and Shi, Y. (2012) *Softboiled Speech: A Contrastive Analysis of Death Euphemisms in Egyptian Arabic and Chinese.* "Global Journal of Human Social Science", 12 (8). https://globaljournals.org/item/445-softboiled-speech-a-contrastive-analysis-of-death-euphemisms-in-egyptian-arabic-and-chinese. Access: July 2021.
Górska, E. (2015). *Intensyfikacja treści we współczesnym arabskim języku literackim.* Kraków: Księgarnia Akademicka.
Grice, H.P. (1975). *Logic and conversation.* [In:] *Speech Acts.* P. Cole and J.L. Morgan (eds.). New York: Academic Press, 41–58.
Grzenia, J. (2006). *Komunikacja językowa w Internecie.* Warszawa: PWN.
Hamady, S. (1960). *Temperament and character of the Arabs.* NY: Twayne Publishers.
Hall, E. (1996). *Northridge Evaluation of Formulas, Idioms and Proverbs in Social Situations.* (NEFIPSS). Unpublished research protocol. Northridge, CA.
Harris, R.M. (1984). *Truth and politeness: a study in the pragmatics of Egyptian Arabic conversation.* University of Cambridge: doctoral dissertation.
Heine, B. (2003). *Grammaticalization.* [In:] *The Handbook of Historical Linguistics.* B.D. Joseph and R.D. Janda (eds.). Oxford: Blackwell, 575–601.
Heine, B. and Reh, M. (1984). *Grammaticalization and reanalysis in African languages.* Hamburg: Buske.
Hidaya, M.O. and Obeidat, H. (2015/2016). *Expressions of Condolence In Algerian Arabic: With Reference to English,* Research project conducted at Yarmouk University. https://www.academia.edu/30918703/Expressions_of_Condolence_In_Algerian_Arabic_With_Reference_to_English. Access: July 2021.
Hofstede, G. (1991). *Culture and Organisations.* New York: McGraw-Hill.
Hopper, P. (1996). *Some recent trends in grammaticalization.* "Annual Review of Anthropology", 25(1), 217–236.

Hughlings Jackson, J. (1874). *On the nature of the duality of the brain.* [In:] *Selected writings of John Hughlings Jackson*, vol. 2, 129–145. J. Taylor (ed.). London: Hodder & Stoughton.

Johnstone Koch, B. (1983). *Presentation as proof. The language of Arabic rhetoric.* Anthropological Linguistics, 25 (1), 47–60.

Jürgens, U. (2002). *Neural pathways underlying vocal control.* "Neuroscience and Biobehavioral Reviews", 26 (2), 235–258.

Khalid, M. (1977). *The sociocultural determinants of Arab diplomacy.* [In:] *Arab and American cultures.* Ed. G.N. Atiyeh. Washington: American Enterprise Institute for Public Research, 123–142.

Kuiper, K. et al. (2007). *Slipping on superlemmas: Multi-word lexical items in speech production.* "The Mental Lexicon", 2 (3), 313–357.

Lancioni, G. (2009). *Formulaic models and formulaicity in Classical and Modern Standard Arabic.* [In:] *Formulaic Language.* Ed. R. Corrigan, E.A. Moravcsik, H. Ouali, K.M. Wheatley. Amsterdam–Philadelphia: John Benjamins Publishing Company.

Lancker, Van, Sidtis, D. (2012a). *Two-Track Mind: Formulaic and Novel Language Support a Dual-Process Model.* [In:] *The Handbook of the Neuropsychology of Language.* Ed. M. Faust. Blackwell Publishing, 342–367.

Lancker, Van, Sidtis, D. (2012b). *Formulaic Language and Language Disorders.* "Annual Review of Applied Linguistics", (32), 62–80.

Leech, G.N. (1983). *Principles of Pragmatics.* London–New York: Longman.

Masliyah, S. (2001). *Curses and insults in Iraqi Arabic.* "Journal of Semitic Studies", XLVI, (2), 267–308.

Mazid, B.E.D.M. (2006). *Translating Emirati Arabic politeness formulas: An exploratory study and a mini-mini-dictionary.* "The 7th annual UAE university research conference". http://static.sdu.dk/mediafiles//E/6/5/%7BE65A230F-0CE1-468C-9150 2E8086E3A1D2%7DBahaa-Eddin%20M.%20Mazid,%2063-85.pdf.

Meillet, A. (1912). *L'evolution des formes grammaticales: Linguistique Historique et Linguistique Generale* (1982), Paris, Champion, 130–148.

Milewski, T. (1965). *Językoznawstwo.* Warszawa: PWN.

Morkus, N. (2014). *Refusals in Egyptian Arabic and American English.* "Journal of Pragmatics", 70, 86–107.

Nazzal, A. (2005). *The Pragmatic Functions of the Recitation of Qur'anic Verses by Muslims in their Oral Genre: The Case of Insha'Allah, 'God's Willing'.* "Pragmatics: Quarterly Publication of the International Pragmatics Association" (IPrA), 15 (2–3), 251–273.

Nelson, L. et al. (1989). *Development and validation of the Neuropsychology Behavior and Affect Profile.* "Journal of Consulting and Clinical Psychology", (1), 266–272.

Noori, B. (2012). *A Pragmatic Analysis of Polite Forms in English and Arabic. A Contrastive Study.* University of Baghdad College: Al-Ustah, 2 (203), 75–85.

Nydell, M. (1987). *Understanding Arabs: A guide for Westerners.* Yarmouth, ME: Intercultural Press.

Parkinson, D.B. (1985). *Constructing the Social Context of Communication: Address in Egyptian Arabic.* Berlin–New York–Amsterdam: Mouton de Gruyter.

Patai, R. (1973). *The Arab Mind.* New York: Scribner.

Pawley, A. (1991). *How to talk cricket: on linguistic competence in a subject matter.* [In:] *Currents in Pacific linguistics: papers on Austronesian languages and ethnolinguistics in honour of George W. Grace.* R. Blust (ed.). Canberra: Pacific Linguistics C-117, 339–368.

Pawley, A. and Syder, F.H. (1983). *Two puzzles for linguistic theory: nativelike selection and nativelike fluency.* [In:] *Language and communication.* J.C. Richards and R.W. Schmidt (eds.). New York: Longman, 191–226.

Perkins, M.R. (1999). *Productivity and formulaicity in language development.* [In:] *Issues in normal & disordered child language: from phonology to narrative. Special Issue of The New Bulmershe Papers.* M. Garman, C. Letts, B. Richards, C. Schelletter and S. Edwards (eds.). Reading: University of Reading, 51–67.

Piamenta, M. (1979). *Islam in Everyday Arabic Speech.* Leiden: E. J. Brill.

Prensky, M. (2001). *Digital Natives, Digital Immigrants.* "On the Horizon" (MCB University Press), 9 (5), 1–6.

Robertson-Smith, W. (1894). *Lectures on the Religion of the Semites (second edition).* London: Adam and Charles Black.

Qanbar, N. (2011). *A Sociolinguistic Study of the linguistic Taboos in the Yemeni Society.* "Modern Journal of Applied Linguistics", 3 (2/3), 86–104.

Salomond, A. (1974). *Rituals of encounter among the Maori.* [In:] *Explorations in the ethnography of speaking.* R. Bauman and J. Sherzer (eds.). London–New York: Cambridge University Press. 192–212.

Sawalmeh, M.H.M. (2019). *Rhetorical Structure and Sociocultural Analysis of Muslim and Christian Obituaries in Jordanian Newspapers* "International Journal of Arabic-English Studies", 19(2), 321–338.

Sinclair, J. McH. (1991). *Corpus, concordance, collocation.* Oxford: Oxford University Press.

Sidtis, D., Canterucci, G. and Katsnelson, D. (2009). *Effects of neurological damage on production of formulaic language.* "Clinical Linguistics and Phonetics", 23 (4), 270–284.

Sperber, D. and Wilson, D. (1987/1996). *Précis of Relevance: communication and cognition.* "Behavioral and Brain Sciences", 10 (4), 697–710. [Reprinted in:] (1996). *Readings in language and mind.* H. Geirsson and M. Losonsky (eds.). Cambridge, MA: Blackwell, 460–486.

Steiner, F. (1967). *Taboo.* London: Penguin Books.

Stewart, D. J. (1996). *Root-Echo Responses in Egyptian Arabic Politeness Formulae.* [In:] *Understanding Arabic. Essays in Contemporary Arabic Linguistics in Honor of El-Said Badawi.* E.-S.M. Badawi, A. Elgibali (eds.). Cairo: The American University in Cairo Press.

Stewart, D. J. (1997). *Impoliteness Formulae: The Cognate Curse in Egyptian Arabic.* "Journal of Semitic Studies", 42 (2), 327–360.

Stewart, D. J. (2014). *Cognate and Analogical Curses in Moroccan Arabic: A Comparative Study of Arabic Speech Genres.* "Arabica", 61 (6), 697–745.

Swinney, D.A. and Cutler, A. (1979). *The access and processing of idiomatic expressions.* "Journal of Verbal Learning and Verbal Behavior", 18 (5), 523–534.

Watts, R.J. (2003). *Politeness.* Cambridge: Cambridge University Press.

Wilmsen, D. (2010). *Understatement, Euphemism, and Circumlocution in Egyptian Arabic: Cooperation in Conversational Dissembling.* [In:] *Information Structure in Spoken Arabic.* J. Owens and A. El Gibaly (eds.). London: Routledge, 243–259.

Winner, E. and Gardner, H. (1977). *The comprehension of metaphor in brain-damaged patients.* "Brain: a Journal of Neurology", 100 (4), 717–729.

Woidich, M. (1995). *Some Cases of Grammaticalization in Egyptian Arabic.* Proceedings of the 2nd International Conference of l'AIDA, Trinity: University of Cambridge.

Woidich, M. (2018). *On some intensifiers in Egyptian Arabic Slang* [In:] *Mélanges offerts à Madiha Doss. La linguistique comme engagement.* A. Boucherit, H. Machhour and M. Rouchdy (eds.). Le Caire: IFAO, 253–273.

Wood, D. (2015). *Fundamentals of formulaic language: An introduction.* London: Bloomsbury.

Wray, A. (2000). *Holistic utterances in protolanguage: The link from primates to humans.* [In:] *The Evolutionary emergence of language: Social function and the origins of linguistic form.* C. Knight, J.R. Hurford and M. Studdert-Kennedy (eds.). Cambridge: Cambridge University Press. 285–302.

Wray, A. (2002). *Formulaic language and the lexicon.* Cambridge: Cambridge University Press.

Wray, A. and Perkins, M. (2000). *The functions of formulaic language: An integrated model.* "Language & Communication", 20 (1), 1–28.

Yahya, E.M. (2010). *A Study of Condolences in Iraqi Arabic with Reference to English.* "Adab Al-rafidayn", (57), 47–70.

Yassin, M.A.F. (1977a). *Bi-polar Kinship Terms of Address in Kuwaiti Arabic.* "Bulletin of the School of Oriental and African Studies", 40, 297–301.

Yassin, M.A.F. (1977b). *Kinship Terms in Kuwaiti Arabic.* "Anthropological Linguistics", 19, 126–132.

Yassin, M.A.F. (1978). *Personal Names of Address in Kuwaiti Arabic.* "Anthropological Linguistics", 20, 53–63.

Zawrotna, M. (2018). *Taboo-based intensifiers in Arabic and Polish.* "Folia Orientalia", (1), 181–197.

Editor
Agnieszka Stęplewska

Technical editor
Joanna Bilmin-Odrowąż

Proofreader
Katarzyna Borzęcka

Typesetter
Paweł Noszkiewicz

Jagiellonian University Press
Editorial Offices: Michałowskiego 9/2, 31-126 Kraków
Phone: +48 12 663 23 80

GPSR Authorized Representative: Easy Access System Europe, Mustamäe tee 50, 10621 Tallinn, Estonia, gpsr.requests@easproject.com

www.ingramcontent.com/pod-product-compliance
Lightning Source LLC
Chambersburg PA
CBHW052144070326
40689CB00051B/3439
* 9 7 8 8 3 2 3 3 5 0 3 1 6 *